BITE
ON PERSONAL
DEVELOPMENT

Fresh thoughts on personal development
with a sharp twist of reality

Phil Murray

Hodder & Stoughton

Copyright © 1997 by Phil Murray
Inside illustration by Kevin Ash

First published in Great Britain in 1997 by Perfect Words and Music
Published in 1999 by Hodder and Stoughton
A division of Hodder Headline PLC

The right of Phil Murray to be identified as the Author of the Work has been asserted by him in accordance with the Copyright, Designs and Patents Act 1998.

10 9 8 7 6 5 4 3 2 1

All rights reserved. No part of this publication may be reproduced, stored in a retrieval system, or transmitted, in any form or by any means without the prior written permission of the publisher, nor be otherwise circulated in any form of binding or cover other than that in which it is published and without a similar condition including this condition being imposed on the subsequent purchaser.

A CIP catalogue record for this title is available from the British Library.

ISBN 0 340 71793 9

Printed and bound in Great Britain by
Mackays of Chatham plc, Chatham, Kent

Hodder and Stoughton
A division of Hodder Headline PLC
338 Euston Road
London NW1 3BH

Love
is
the
only
revolution

This book is dedicated to
human potential
successful transformation
and
the only revolution.

Should You Buy This Book?

This book contains fresh thoughts with a sharp twist of reality on the popular theme of personal development. It disseminates a viewpoint that all beliefs are mental and spiritual straight-jackets ... the days of the guru are over and that any teacher who leaves you with a feeling of dependence on that teacher, is a charlatan, a fake, a fraud and perhaps naively all three

Phil writes that ... Quality will remain as does a hanging note of music drifting into eternity ... his often poetic style is uncompromising however, when it comes to dealing with aspects of the so called new age ... Just as money inflow is a by-product of commercially oriented service, so too are abilities, awareness and true human progress all by-products of the simple service of humanity by an individual.

If you want back-slapping ... if you are happy in your comfort-zone ... if you think that your god is better than everyone else's and anti social diseases can only be remedied in the special clinic of a hospital ... place this book back on the shelf and choose another.

Which road do you want to travel? The well worn route which most take because it is easy? The path shown to you by your socialisation process? The way society goes with trends, fads, gimmicks and gizmos? Or will you take the road less well travelled, which is maintained by the few, for the many who inevitably will follow?

If you join with Phil on this trip then it is doubtful that you will ever be the same again.

ALL THE TIME YOU ARE BELIEVING IN SOMETHING, YOU ARE LESS SENSITIVE TO LIFE

Contents

please read all of the following bites at random and according to your feelings for their relevance to your process

A First Bite ... *introduction*
Abilities Awareness Aha
After Before The Beginning Is A Thought
And So On And So Forth
Anti Social Diseases
Art And Personal Development
an interview with the artist
Bite Right Into the Pie
Books
Dear John
Fact And Inspiration
From Russia With Grief
Governments
Guarantees
Gurus
Happiness
Honesty
Humanimal
In What Should We All Believe
Jesus Christ And The Christians
Letter From America
Life In The Day Of
Little Billy And The Big Heavy
London
Mordy Visits The Islands
Mr Mire
My Personal Story ... *so far*
NLP And All That
Performance And You At The Half Way Mark

POLITICS
POOR NOT SO POOR AND POOREST
RELATIONSHIPS
RESPONSIBILITY
SALLY
SIGH
SILENT KNIGHT PHILOSOPHY AND PERSONAL DEVELOPMENT
an interview with a Silent Knight
SMILE
SPECIAL OFFERS
SPEED LIMITS
SPONTANEOUS DISCUSSION
SPOT CARPENTER THE FISH MAN
STITCH IN TIME
STORYTELLING AND PERSONAL DEVELOPMENT
an interview with The Storyteller
TAKE A BREAK AND RECREATE
TASTE
TELEPATHY AND PSYCHIC AURAS
TELEVISION TELEPHONE RADIO AND THE INTERNET
THE EVIL OF PSYCHO SURGERY
THE HAUNTING OF CYRUS HIVANTREE
THE ONE ABOUT WHOM IT IS FUTILE TO SPECULATE
THE THING ABOUT WHICH IT IS EXCITING TO SPECULATE
VACATIONS
WHAT DOES BEING POSITIVE REALLY MEAN?
WHAT IS *THE LIGHT?*
WHO IS YOUR DOCTOR?
WHY ARE SO MANY OF US SKINT?
WORDS AND LANGUAGE
YOU AND SERENDIPITY
YOU CAN ALWAYS GET WHAT YOU WANT TOO

A First Bite
introduction

What can a book of this type accomplish for you? Where can new ideas take you? How can bites of data aid personal development? When is it appropriate to surround yourself with inspiration? Can there be more to life than meets the eye?

This book will pose more questions for you than it will give answers! If it is an easy ride to glory which you seek, this is not the vehicle which will take you there. There is a noticeable absence of backslapping contained herein, and a more effective search for meaning. This is accomplished because the author has constantly sought to reveal the truth which exists behind what is more readily available to us all as sensational headlines, buzz words, fashionable statements about human capabilities and slick phrases revealing nothing but empty promises of a free ride to nowhere at someone else's expense.

The cost of this honesty and refusal to go *the way of the world*, is a less commercially viable book and a simultaneous disregard by the mass media of its contribution to the pool of creative thought which has ever brought home to the human race a taste of its real potential.

I have sold many thousands of books and tapes; they have changed lives and helped readers and listeners effect *self realisations,* which I understand to be the only way forward for true progress. There are however, many more people seeking authors, gurus and presenters who promise them advancement through mere association with the personalities and products involved. This book is not for those people yet, it is written for those of us willing to get into action and take responsibility for ourselves.

You will find little information on the following pages; rather, interwoven between stories, facts and observations, is an interesting and effective way of looking at life, revealing the potential application of all experience to personal achievement, with consequent universal gain, as it is believed that adoption of a positive mental attitude by an individual has strong beneficial effects on all around the user of that mind frame.

So, as you are still reading the introduction, welcome to BITES ON PERSONAL DEVELOPMENT. I hope you find this collection of titles just right to impel you into a process which will allow ever more constant personal cognitions on who and what you really are. If not, put the book to one side, then retrieve it during a moment when the words feel more relevant to the particular process in life you are undergoing at that time.

Warm thoughts from not too far away ... *Phil Murray*

ABILITIES AWARENESS AHA

I have been in the fortunate position for most of my adult life, to have lived around people who have pursued human potential in all its various guises, and with assorted degrees of success. This has been the case to such an extent that I began investigation into the worth of such endeavour. I have watched people use religion to further their own ends, observed others practising mantras, raja yoga and meditation to grope in the general direction of success, whilst friends have also contemplated past lives in an effort to unclog the mysteries of this life.

I have done many of these things myself! The distinction which is missing from most such activity is that which exists between human life and the spiritual existence. Failure to differentiate between these two aspect of living, render all endeavour into the realms of human potential almost invalid. A small advance here and a little profit there are possible for sure, but nothing like the gain aspirations of most individuals I know can be met.

If you want to learn tricks of the personal development world from the industry angle, you attend vastly overpriced seminars which encourage you to awaken the unlimited potential which lurks within us all, by adopting a number of habits which highly effective people apparently utilise. Yet, the spiritual part of your inherent duality will rarely, if ever, be addressed. Smile training may be instructed, customer relations will be glossed over ... *the bosses like this one at the moment,* affirmations regarding the unlocking of more personal energy for input into the business which sent you there in the first place will be evident, breaking through mental barriers and getting physically fit may also form part of a course.

Conversely, there are people who attend religious oriented retreats, who relax and contact areas of their personal universe seemingly unavailable to them during the course of their normal life, yet they feel unable to apply this sensation effectively to this normal life which must ultimately occupy most of their incarnation.

Then there are those of us who seek new and more powerful general abilities, strikingly awesome and ubiquitous awareness, *of what I do not know,* and before you know it you're hooked. Awareness? Abilities? Aha! Gotcha! Every time there is a personal aim for the sake of it, progress is limited to the results of gimmick oriented stimulus. Yet, whatever is required by an individual in the honourable service of fellow humanity, be it as a shop assistant or messiah, will be forthcoming naturally, and in exact ratio, to that requirement.

Awareness and abilities arise within an individual as a by-product of service. Just as an apprentice plumber habitually and effectively inculcates himself with knowledge to the degree he is around the application of such knowledge, so does a spiritual being incarnated on this planet, inculcate itself with relevant data and intuition. In other words, people who meditate, begin to understand meditation. Those who work with finance daily, become experts in the money markets; artists paint, musicians play, writers write and thespians act!

Am I stating the obvious? I ask that question in anticipation of your contemplation of it! Yes. We tend to often overlook the observable evidence however. I have a friend who speaks of her oil painting aspirations. I asked if she currently painted, to which she replied in the negative. *Painters paint,* I concluded. You can only improve in anything by a constant association with it. The challenge we face in the personal development world is however, that of furthering the mental horizons without alienating the pupils. You cannot address the spiritual side of a person effectively, if that person has not encountered it prior to your discourse, unless your role is helping such contact. Likewise, a spiritual person may have little inclination in the commercial world of industry, until introduced to the spiritual challenges discoverable therein.

My work hopefully sits on that line which can be metaphorically drawn between the two aspects of duality evident in physical incarnation. It is an invitation to cross over from wherever you are now, to the other side, without really leaving anything behind. It is an exploration of the potential embrace of all aspects of earthly existence and beyond. In BEFORE THE BEGINNING IS A THOUGHT, I described it as ...

WHAT WHY AND WHEN
The path of Personal Development is as long as you wish.
Half way along that length another Path can be seen. This
route will take you all the distance that you would have

travelled had you remained on the path of Personal Development, and then further.

Some stay on the first path and flourish. Others stay on the first path, flourish, and wonder what it's like on the other Path they can see running parallel to the one on which they travel. Some cross over too soon onto the other way and are not prepared for the nature of this route less well travelled.

Others follow my golden rule of *Gradual Graduation*.

I believe in Personal Development.

I believe in the encouragement of *Private Victory*.

I also believe that this type of victory can atrophy ... unless transformed into *Public Victory*.

Ultimate Victory is *Service*.

First published as the Foreword to Before the Beginning Is A Thought, 1994.

Just as money inflow is a by-product of commercially oriented service, so too are abilities, awareness and true human progress all by-products of the simple service of humanity by an individual. Do not make that human error in thinking that all such service need be headline grabbing, because the opposite is normal.

AFTER BEFORE THE BEGINNING IS A THOUGHT

Thought got us where we are today, but sure as eggs is eggs it will not take us where we wish to dwell tomorrow! Human thought is responsible for the miserable and logical conditions which we find globally spreading still at alarming rates. It is incapable of serving us graciously into the finer aspects of life, which can be sensed by an ever increasing number of creative people, who realise that the moment thought is applied to intuitively understood new horizons, demotion of a beautiful concept is the result.

Before human thought was available to us, our physical primogenitors were capable only of an instinctual approach to life, much as some of our more advanced animals are today. *Hunger equalled eat ... anger equalled repel ... pain equalled something to be avoided ... stimulus equalled response.*

As we have progressed with the help of thought, we may now like to contemplate an evolutionary bounce towards intuition; *instinct ... thought ... intuition,* is the emerging pattern which has been deemed part of The Plan for the human race.

I have always affirmed that there are many paradoxes and downright contradictions in this personal development world, and I hope those of you who spent the time reading or listening to my second book called BEFORE THE BEGINNING IS A THOUGHT, do not think it any less relevant now than when first it was studied. It is a step in my approach to self improvement. Can you imagine the ensuing anarchy resultant from a sudden understanding of reincarnation by the masses. Those less scrupulous than desirable would perhaps take greater risks with their crimes; life would be much cheaper; populations far more difficult to control; religions would be dumped; guidelines scrapped and corporal punishment celebrated!

Gradual Graduation is ever the rule. As this is the case, we must celebrate the sudden cognition by many that YOU CAN ALWAYS GET WHAT YOU WANT, before it dawns on those same people that BEFORE THE BEGINNING IS A THOUGHT, which may find them seeking spiritual EMPOWERMENT, to realising that stories in THE 49 STEPS TO A BRIGHT LIFE perhaps explain a relevance in their urging for each of us to discover and live our own personal and unique legends. These BITES ON PERSONAL DEVELOPMENT seem to create another route available to us for an even greater insight into who, what and why we are.

Thought relegates all it contemplates to the level of that thought's quality. Yet, those of us with little thought power may have access to a plane of potential far in advance of the Mental Universe which I discuss so frequently and passionately. The Intuitive Planes of existence and contemplation are there for us all to access as and when an appropriate ability is achieved. It therefore follows that to judge one seemingly lacking in thought power, is exceedingly dangerous and utterly futile, as you will only ever be capable of contemplating that individual's assets through your own thoughts, which themselves are incapable of the necessary intuition to assess an accurate reading.

Where do all these words verging on the gobbledegook leave us? Hopefully, with an expanded intelligence capable of thinking beyond itself. It is almost as if the mind has to perceive something greater than intellect, and allow us to aspire towards it with the ultimate sacrifice by thought of dying as a result. Well, this seems to fall into an evolutionary pattern now doesn't it!

For the time being though, it is the case that we all must utilise both thought and intuition, until the latter dominates the former, which will eventually fade into obscurity. From a practical viewpoint on a global level, successful negotiators of peace to end any conflict, are those who perhaps quite unwittingly, cease to allow logical thought to dominate, and allow an inspiration of intuition to lift their contemplations beyond what would make further war inevitable. This is why I describe the need for *extraordinary efforts to utilise experience of a different nature; an inherent experience born of compassion and desire for us all to live side by side in harmony,* in anyone's search for peaceful solutions to anything.

It is very difficult for most of us to understand the *before the beginning is a thought* philosophy as essentially a tool for the service of others. The immediate human response is to conceive of something that individual wants, contemplate it through and wait for it to physically happen. This works, but it is in the utilisation of extraordinary means which we are calling intuition, that real power is sensed. It is in using the intuitive plane, and inspiration from this level, that soul purpose swings into being, lighting up all that lines its path.

Before anyone becomes involved in this type of contemplation, it must be considered whether or not that individual wishes upheaval to an otherwise orderly life. The moment contemplations stray from the norm, is the cosmic instant that individual begins sensing that there is more to life than meets the eye.

Use thought as an instrument of living, but always keep it inspired from a higher level. Do not ever let thought think you, because it has a strange habit of making you think that you are thinking thoughts which in fact thought is thinking for you! The brain is the physical organ which allows a spirit having a human experience to manifest thought; Ambrose Bierce described the brain as *an apparatus with which we think that we think*. It is in fact an apparatus which we *use* to think that we think, when in fact we could use it to think that we do not need to think ... *quite so much!*

Before the beginning is a thought, and the sole purpose of that contemplation is creation. After thought has been explored and utilised, you may contemplate transcending the medium. In order to accomplish this you must become better acquainted with yourself during increasing moments of silence, stillness and solitude, otherwise known as TTM, an acronym for *Time To Myself,* and meditation. This is the only way forward of which I am currently aware. The exercise is free of financial involvement and can be accomplished in a variety of locations, as long as they are quiet and you can be alone, unless engaged with others in group meditations.

You must be willing to accept the sudden dawning of ideas, unexpected concepts, inexplicable viewpoints and a whole host of other phenomena which words cannot describe. Please do not seek sensation or sensationalism. Personal happenings need not be related and if nothing happens for you that is as good as anything else occurring.

Meditation is just being, and just being happens after before the beginning is a thought, *I feel!*

AND SO ON AND SO FORTH

I flagrantly refuse to ever deliver or accept such indistinctions as this title surely is, in communications to or from anywhere, anyone and about anything. A neurosis of our time is the lack of ability and determination, to conclude a communication as you intend it, without leaving the latter part of it totally open to interpretation and misinterpretation; frequently the latter!

Speech and the written word are direct reflections of what is less visible inside your own personal universe. They are an effort to join your invisible side through a mutually agreeable medium, with the invisible side of another; otherwise you would just stand and be looked at for another to judge you, or manifest some mannerism relevant to your intended meaning. If you are not able to verbally compose your communications accurately, then why should the recipient be expected to think for you by guessing at your meaning.

Etc etc is an often utilised locution designed to ease the strain of the instigator at the expense of the recipient. What does it mean?

It can be interpreted as laziness, lack of integrity, not knowing yourself what comes next, or worse still, an effort to make the recipient think you know more than in fact you do know!

Do you know what I mean is another culprit. Frequently shortened in an endeavour to ease the verbal workload even further for the instigator to, *know what I mean;* this is a shoddy effort to warmly include the recipient deeply, in a friendly way, with your emanation, which must have been explained with little clarity if this question needs to be asked so quickly after the initial statement has been posed.

Blah blah blah, usually signifies that correctly wording the remainder of a story would be more boring than writing or saying these three meaningless and asseverating blots of blandness. I don't think so.

Communication of every type is a unique method of linking up, be it by medium of a meditative glance, the written word, oral utterance or any of many other communication methods less relevant to this bite. You must understand that whatever you are thinking at a particular time, is exactly what you are. Verbal emanations are representations of your thoughts, and offer an easy way for someone to determine your qualities. Is it not therefore worth your while to firstly think the right thoughts, but secondly and more relevant to this topic, write and speak in a way which is suitable for interpretation as to who and what you really are.

Whilst we are discussing this subject, may I also remind regular readers of my work, and perhaps introduce others for the first time to, the idea that your mental lexicon is a direct trailblazer for your ability to grasp new concepts. It is these new ideas which allow you to personally develop beyond the norm of your contemporaries, by presenting glimpses of new horizons previously veiled until a new word or phrase opens them up for you.

There are perhaps, two words already in this bite which are not commonly used in everyday situations ... *locution and asseverating*. If you have passed them without understanding what they are intended to convey, then, after clearing their definitions precisely utilising a good dictionary, make a note of this shortcoming and encourage yourself away from such habit.

Once you have cognited on wordpower, you may then enjoy contemplation of a wordless world where concepts are too fine and filled with nuance for our language medium to describe. In so doing you may find yourself receptive to self realisation of an intuitive nature. All methods of self improvement are worthy if they are good for others and yourself.

Any generality will eventually rebound negatively onto you with the power you were seeking to gain through the use of vagueness. Be wary of collective nouns and pronouns such as *people* and *they*. There are times when such words are relevant of course, but I am urging you not to use them when they are a substitute for more detail. The advertising media thrives on groupings of just about every description ... *people love ... dogs just adore ... the English are ... wise people buy ... men need ... they know best ... women should.*

Generalities have a nasty habit of hooking you into certain feelings which are not necessarily your own; this is why the advertising agencies utilise vagueness whenever it is assessed powerful for the attraction of more sales ... whether or not purchasers actually need or want the advertised items!

I urge you to be yourself at all times; *know what I mean*. Fight the good fight, *etc etc,* and remember the story of the man who, well, you know the rest ... *blah blah blah. They* don't like it you know, and *people* should always have *one* when *that time* is at hand. Always concentrate on the improvement of what I mentioned plus more, *and so on and so forth!*

You do know what I mean, *don't you?*

ANTI SOCIAL DISEASES

Venereal disease, scabies, fungal smells, herpes, athletes foot, genital discharges, halitosis, worms, ugliness and scabs, all pale into considerable insignificance when compared to a malaise which has swept civilisation since thinking began. It is an illness encouraged by doctors, dentists, therapists, new age workshops, religions, beliefs, cults, sects, families and friends alike. It creeps upon an individual during the socialisation process of growing up, during which time it is at its most virulent and contagious. The disease leaves a sufferer and those around the afflicted, confused, sad, melancholic and introverted; occasionally violence is a symptom, along with a yearning for totally new surroundings.

If you were confronted with a disease as described above, perhaps encouraged by the popular press and supported by armies of do-gooders collecting hand-outs at main line railway stations, would you not join hands to accelerate the eradication of such a viperous and insidious virus?

I wonder what you are expecting to read next ... a name for this disease ... a cure ... the culprits ... a continuous tirade ...

DUPLICITY is an apt word to summarise this saddest of human conditions which I describe. What does the word mean? Duplicity means *deceit, artifice, cunning, wile, speaking with forked tongue* and *double dealing*. I define it as *bi-directional intention*. In short, one may immediately identify an experience of it by recalling a time when you have said one thing and meant another;

alternatively, by remembering a time when you know another duped you in a similar fashion.

The frequency which duplicity has now managed to manifest itself in our lives, makes it more virulent than The Plague and a larger compounding contributing factor to the scale of human misery than any one single episode in most physical incarnations.

It is no use pretending that it will be easy to eradicate from our lives because it is so deeply rooted into our habits and actions, that to make a sudden withdrawal from its utilisation, would cause more damage to relationships, interdependancies and friendships than would be tolerable. You have to adopt my *Gradual Graduation* policy when deciding to remove duplicity from your modus operandi. Do it *bit by bit!*

Encouragers of duplicity will describe situations where it is kinder to lie than tell the truth. Your mother gets on your nerves but you do not dare tell her so or why, because she couldn't take it. It is likely *you* who cannot manage to confront the issue I reckon. More often than not, the potential recipients of the truth you cannot bear to utter, have survived a world war or two, brought a few children the physical opportunity of conscious existence on this planet, run a house and home, held down a job, created their own lives through much adversity, and yet we so often feel that they will not be able to suffer a simple truth.

Let me tell you, it is the lie they cannot suffer; the duplicitous bending of the truth into an unpalatable portion of sickness. Whether you acknowledge it or not, the vast majority of people who are recipients of duplicity, know it is happening, but, continuing the malaise, they dare not tell the bringer of lies lest it upset the liar!

You may gather now, the extent of the damage already done,

when sufferers protect their inflicters. When you have noticed that a neighbour's attitude is less friendly than it was, and you ask if all is well, to receive an affirmative answer, this neighbour has missed the golden opportunity to relate perhaps a simple upset about a garden boundary or an overheard noise.

Bi-directional intentioned outflow produces bi-directional intentioned inflow into your universe, and life becomes diluted into a weak harmonic of its potential.

The cure begins with an aim to have duplicity removed from the dictionary, or at the very least have it demoted to the description of *obsolete*. You must firstly cognite on the damage it is doing to yourself and surrounding society. Then you may feel able to communicate that you are predisposed to hear truth at all times, even when it is hurtful. Discovering some close contemporaries who may be amenable to the sharing of this experience, may prove fruitful if you are to discover willing recipients of a truth emanation from yourself.

First encounters may lead us into murky waters, as the pressure valve is opened and we find an outlet for our pent-up feelings and unsaids. The unscrupulous amongst us of course, will see any move to eradicate duplicity, as a unique opportunity for a barrage of suppressive communications intent on clubbing you down to the ground in screams of pain.

It is a long term personal development target I describe here. The gratification may be deferred, and the treatment could feel like a short sharp shock. *Hold the vision and maintain the drive.* The short term effect will find your colleagues begin to describe you as safe, honest and, hurtful but truthful sometimes. The medium term will be a period of accelerated growth enabled by the fact that you know exactly what is your position regarding others, rather than misunderstanding communications resulting in half cocked plans and expectations. Eventually the rose will show itself, and your personal development will have had that ripple effect so often described as potent when used for good.

We give up smoking, cut down on alcohol, stop eating sweets and chocolates, lose weight, cease swearing, think positively, act kindly ... and now I invite you to cease duplicity in all its ugly guises, with the affirmation ... I MEAN WHAT I SAY AND SAY WHAT I MEAN!

ART AND PERSONAL DEVELOPMENT
an interview with the artist

Phil Murray
What is the relationship between art and personal development?

The artist
I feel the true nature of art, is *to reveal* that which lies deep within human divinity. It is through the images we contemplate, that we become. For me, art has a significant role to play in influencing, aligning or reflecting, the whole of human nature; subjectively and objectively. Its highest potential is to lead humanity away from *the shackles that bind,* in order to awaken each person's real self ... *to uplift the downcast eyes unto the sun.* The ultimate possibility of personal development is no different to this vision; to feed the individual's inner life and to engage all in the creative and spiritual process of living.

Phil Murray
Is art a therapy within itself?

The artist
If the definition of therapy is, *a curative treatment,* then from my own personal experience I would say *yes* to this question; but only

if the underlying intention is founded upon the principles I described in my answer to the previous question. If illness is a result of lost alignment with the whole of our self, then the creative process can serve as a vehicle which restores our balance. It is through this creative process that the depth of our nature is revealed and experienced. This understanding does not come from a process of *thinking* before *creating*. It arrives in an individual universe, like a flower mysteriously emerging from the earth itself. We create in order to understand.

Phil Murray
Is there such a distinction as good and bad art; do good and bad people, *(forgive the description)* react differently to art?

The artist
Increasingly, I like to refrain from using such terms as good and bad. I look upon people and art as being in different stages of growth. When one stands back to look at a bigger picture of humanity's evolution, and therefore the evolution of art, one sees a tapestry being woven. Each thread has a different colour and quality; the image of this picture is dependent on our choices. Hopefully, the images we contemplate in our lives, and from generation to generation, will eventually reveal a truly great work of art. Cecil Collins once said that ... *a painting is often just a series of choices, but a truly great work of art is a gift from God.*

Phil Murray
Why are you an artist?

The artist
I am an artist because I have the gift of being able to paint, and a desire to help humanity. To begin with, I became an artist in order to heal myself, and to contact a higher aspect of my human nature. This aspect was hidden behind worldly desires and fears. As I painted images which held within them my deepest wish to live the *beauty within,* without fear, it became. At that point the question

arose ... *what am I to do with this?* In time, it became clear to me that the greatest service that I, Ginger Gilmour, could offer humanity, was to use my natural talent to create a *vision of the future,* which would aid in the transfiguration of human consciousness.

> Many can choose to stay within the Maya
> Many can choose to heal the wounds.
> Some can choose to create a vision for the future
> which will set the bound heart of humanity free.
> I have chosen to participate in the latter ...
> *to listen, remember and create.*

Phil Murray
Are your paintings a representation of you *the being*, in any way, shape or form?

The artist
I feel that what we are, is always reflected in our art and lives. My vision is to serve the highest aspect that we can be as human beings. My hope is that this will come through into my life and into my art. My greatest wish is to offer every individual a moment of inspiration, which allows them to touch that divinity we all possess. What a different world the earth would be if all of us aspired to live *the beauty which we truly are*.

Phil Murray
How can we all learn to live our own personal art form more accurately, and with less influence from external stimuli?

The artist
One thought which has served me most on my journey has been to trust and to focus on my *vision*. It is the quality, the holding and the mastery of my intent, that has influenced my process more than any other aspect. Often a voice of encouragement from a friend would say ... *Ginger, believe in your vision.* Believing in the truth of my

intent to live my vision, influenced me more than the individual interpretations or responses. With regard to influence from external stimuli, it has often been my experience, that some days one can be a saint, and other days a devil, in the eyes of many. More and more I have learned not to identify with these external reactions as being the nature of my vision, or to depend on them in order for my vision to exist, but see them as helpful hints as to what is my next step in the process of living a vision ... a vision to live creatively with the soul's intention in this human body. Often this vision can stir mud, so that the pool can clear within myself and others. This is part of the process. I now spend most of the time developing and living my vision. There are lots of tests along the way which I prefer thinking of as *opportunities* to discover more of my essential nature. I seek to live a vision of *freedom* beyond all influences and conditionings known to man ... but in so doing, I have had also to find a way of existing alongside others who seek to live and believe something different. What has helped, is the knowledge that we are all on the same journey, but each of us treads a different path ... each specially designed with the highest in mind for all.

Phil Murray
Do you feel that art is the soul of the planet?

The artist
If the language of art is based on a concept of the Divine, then I would say that it *is* the soul of the planet. Most modern art is involved with images that are more concerned with the thesis *art for art's sake*. For me this is only part of the picture. Aesthetics by themselves, outside the context of the whole, holds little meaning for me within the process of what is truly a reality of humanity's nature and creation. For art to be the soul of the planet and for an artist to reflect this quality, I feel it necessary to ponder the underlying premise ... *man is a metaphysical being, and therefore, art is a metaphysical experience.*

Phil Murray
Thank you ...

The artist
You're welcome

the artist is Ginger Gilmour

BITE RIGHT INTO THE PIE

The subject of beliefs and opinions is perhaps the single most effective discussion point we can manifest in this day and age. It is the most challenging, frightening and enlightening topic, which we all must encounter on our climb up the ladder. Just about every aspect of life is met with beliefs of some kind or other; they act as a buffer between physical life and the spiritual helmsperson. Lazy writers pounce upon them for the purpose of exploitation and easy pickings; in so doing they pick up many followers and drifters eager to have an even easier time of it by allowing others to formulate their useless beliefs for them.

Believers in personal development are often the toughest, and in the case of this topic, the least inspirational people with which to hold such discussion. I know because I was one of them! If you have just learned a new trick which has the apparency of bettering your life, you are not likely to give it up without a fight. Yet, the only good that ever came from any such trick is a cognition, or self realisation, and once that new horizon has been understood, the trick ceases to have any use for you whatsoever.

Just like any physical possession however, new information, personal development data and other people's beliefs which seem to have been useful for them, are cosseted, hoarded, protected and defended. Yet we all know innately that such behaviour is all a complete waste of time and effort. Even the discussion of these cognitions and self realisations that I mention can be damaging, if those listening take them on board as their own without having honestly realised the new horizons within for themselves. Those people are personal development frauds.

If you want to personally develop, one of the biggest steps you can take is to address tired and worn beliefs that are holding you back. Because my brand of personal development straddles the boundaries normally existent betwixt religion and philosophy, self help and imposed education, I encounter many who *turn off*, the moment a topic with which they are not accustomed or comfortable, rears its head. Yet, topics which have this reaction with people are the exact subjects which need to be addressed if those people are to better themselves.

Once you are on the path of self improvement it is unlikely that you will ever step off it. There will be breaks, resting points and plateaux, where achievement may be pondered, but any who try to undermine their own efforts up to a certain point, will always be haunted by the success that those labours have thrown their way. To undermine the haunting will be to give it further power, making recollection of success even more vivid.

This is the way it is! We can work with the natural order of life, or plot against it. We have the sordid ability to upset nature and exhibit *the apparency* of short term gain. Just as the myopic clearing of the rain forests will eventually dawn on the mass of humanity as a gross betrayal of the trust placed with us as guardians of this physical planet, so will the rest of natural philosophy find its place within each and every human heart. It is this same natural philosophy when applied to the mental universe, which shows us that the only real gain we can ever have is that we have sought ourselves.

If you seek more beliefs and opinions then they will surely

come your way. If you would like to explore life without them, this is also possible. The habits which are allowed to profit in the physical world, such as the clearing of these vital rain forests, have a stifling effect on visible nature, including incarnate humanity. Beliefs and opinions have a similar stifling effect in every personal mental universe which accompanies each one of us through this conscious existence. With each discarded belief, a mental tree once more finds life.

Stand free from all superstition, rumour, gossip, opinion and belief; in so doing, you will feel yourself soaring above popular sentiment, which exists for the harnessing of each member of humanity dwelling on it, to a negative existence. Those standing free in such a manner, must not detach themselves from normal life for the sake of it; rather, a new and vibrant outlook will act as an example of living the talk, which is all too rare in this world which we inhabit.

Bite into the personal development pie, live the talk and be a shining example to us all. If you require acknowledgement of any kind you will be disappointed; I therefore urge you not to seek it, more often than not it will then come your way. As outflow equals inflow, so too does the quality of these flows. Bear this in mind when deciding on a course of action. For every action there is a reaction and knowledge of this axiom should shield you from contemplation of any endeavours which are less than scrupulous. I urge you to spend more time discovering *yourself* and all of the qualities that lie within, before seeking qualities and attributes which society has socialised into you as being sought after.

No one knows better than you about you!

Books

It is inevitable, that anyone operating in the publishing business will have a degree of attention on what sells and what flops ... who writes what and what writes who! As I surveyed the contents of one particular large mainstream high street chain bookstore, what jumped out at me was the amount of books *not* written by *professional* authors. Now, this is quite a serious matter, as the content of such book shops determines your breadth of choice in reading material. There is only a very small percentage of readers willing to investigate topics, books and authors not found within their everyday sphere of operation, like easily accessible book outlets which are frequently found within train station newsagents, and the town centre chain stores.

The prompt for this investigation was, that our main chain store customer changed management, increased their discount arbitrarily by another 8%, which is just about our profit margin, and announced that they are about to implement a policy of selling *proven sales only* books in a smaller space within their stores, because profits had fallen due to the demise of the net book agreement, which had up until late 1995 kept book prices artificially high. This means that *other* stores will have to sell the books in the first instance, in order for them to accrue the proven sales, future sales of which will then be creamed of by the store in question.

Here we have a case of crass corporate lack of responsibility, which seems to attack any organisation or individual life, which is run purely for profits, without soul and an absence of heart. It also means that companies like the one which publishes this book may not be considered for stock because we do not generate enough *mass* sales ... we merely provide variety for the discerning buyer! This is dangerous ground my friends! I advise you to consider the implications of such short sighted business sense, not only for the case in point, but also within your own lives.

Do you know what story you wish to tell through living this life? Do you have a plan? Do you have a visualisation statement? Is your life compatible with your written aspirations for it? Do you have a burning desire? Can you encapsulate that longing into one succinct sentence which we can call your mission statement? If not then, I can only surmise that you will be less resourceful than you would be armed with your business card tucked firmly in your mind. You know the type ... *have gun will travel ... if you want it I can sell it to you ... Fafafar's the name, cars are the game.* Or is it ... *give me your cash and I'll spend it!* Without a mission statement you run the risk of drifting with other people's determinism.

The sole fundamental at the base of any mission statement has to be *service!* Providing that this chain of stores makes its myopic mission of *making cash for its stakeholders* known, then no harm is done and we can all make our choice of where to shop based on a truth. How rare such honesty is however. Lip service must be paid to the new fashions of interdependence and service first; this is the beginning of a new cycle of human mistrust.

This book is not the medium for me to discuss the technology of mission statements and service ... that I have already explained in previous books, most especially You Can Always Get What You Want. The reason for this subject raising its head one more time, is that the bookstore in question is plainly lacking any policies of co-operation with its suppliers and its customers, save the policies it gives cant to in its internal magazines which implore sales assistants to bow down before anyone showing a purse and walking in their general direction.

The lack of professional authors visible on the shelves in these stores, is indicative of a malaise which I can only describe as the quickening tide of literary demise. People buy personalities! That is why any book thrown together by a publishing house with a famous name on its cover gets the all important shelf space. One of my favourite footballers was a case in point. He is an artist on the pitch, but in the post match interviews he can barely toss two sentences together without ten *expletives, three over the moons,* six *some you win some you lose,* two *we was better on the day* and seven *sick as a parrots.* His book however, was almost poetic in its style ... I mentioned this to the publishing executive responsible for that particular project, and he became most defensive with regard to my hint at his misrepresentation.

In personal development, we see the same pattern emerging ... great orators throwing books together of their excellent talks, which do not quite make it as written work. Brilliant business trainers, whose work has proven capacity to increase happiness and productivity in the workplace, having ghost writers compile a ghastly weaker version of their otherwise excellent material. Psychologists, who are enjoyable on a one to one basis with their patients, trying unsuccessfully to be just as pleasing with the written word.

Different mediums call for varying skills, in entertainment or any other aspect of society for that matter. Just because a person is good at one aspect of a subject, does not automatically accredit him with the literary know how with which to convey the same sentiments as he has already successfully disseminated orally perhaps, utilising the written word. I believe that if we all concentrate on what each of us is good at and happy with, and leave others to do the same, then *horses for courses,* as my footballing friend would say, we will develop a stronger base from which we can all expand.

So often I am confronted with successful people who moan loudly for a chance to accomplish what they really want to do. My advice is always simple if I feel they are talking about their true raison d'être. Do it! Nothing in this life can be more relevant for any individual than that unique story which is theirs to tell through living. Be true to your life's purpose. Discover *YourStory* before you are *HiStory*.

Do we need a tee shirt for every successful music album ... a film from every good book ... a book from every talented footballer ... an acting performance from every meteorologist. Develop your fundamental purpose and then expand *from* that platform of power. If that expansion is for the sake of money, ego, or a combination of both, then I would once again examine your fundamental purpose for integrity, then honestly judge if you have discovered a glowing note of cosmic awe, or weak harmonics of a dying song.

BRADLEY OF BROADWATER DOWN
THE STORY OF AN OLD SOLDIER

If I said that my experience all those years ago had made life easier, then I would be misleading you. The experience to which I am alluding had resulted in affording me a life of greater interest perhaps, as I never found it possible to pass a dull moment when the potential for contemplation of that experience was possible.

You the reader, will inevitably be expecting some graphic description of this experience which passed my way during the early twentieth century, and if this is so, I fear you may be disappointed with this humble writing, which I promised would occur if I lived to be a hundred years old. I warn you of this possibility at an early stage, that you may read something else more tangible if this is the case, and not waste your time with the written ramblings of an old man.

My name is Harold Pendergrass Bradley, born on the 30th July 1895 to a pair of doting parents, who concluded on my arrival that life centred around their home located in Lansdowne Road, Notting

Hill, London, would not be appropriate for one such as me, and promptly sold up and moved to a beautiful tree lined avenue in Tunbridge Wells, Kent, called Broadwater Down, which they deemed a more gentile and loving environment. I was only five years old when they were both tragically killed in a wholly avoidable accident, when their hansom cab overturned in an effort by the driver to avoid killing a dog which had strayed onto its path.

I was thereafter brought up, looked after, occasionally paraded and regularly pampered, admired, coddled and adored by a variety of relations, parental friends and casual baby-sitters. My rebellion against this upbringing resulted in army enlistment during 1914, to satisfy the purpose of serving my country, which purpose in fact was constitutionally absent within my constitution, making it all the more essential that I should seek it; for my pains I survived the Somme as a witness to the needless death of many dear friends, some of whom I secretly envied in their state of premature departure from this odd life I seemed to be enduring.

It was on the battlefield in the May of 1915 I think, although it may have been 1916, for I was in France three and a half years in all during that war, that I had the first part of my experience, during a bright and full moon; the fighting had been fierce and we had all discussed a particularly nasty and vicious atmosphere over and above that of which we had become accustomed. Suddenly, for no apparent reason, a period of around fifteen minutes silence descended on that field of hatred. A calm during which I have no recollection of any words being exchanged between trench weary soldiers, quite used to passing each day in a burble of busy and nonsensical verbal exchanges about nothing in particular.

Now, I cautioned you at the beginning of this record that I was about to impart quite intangible ideas about an experience I find impossible to describe, and the previous paragraph describes the beginning of it. When I asked my friends afterwards if something happened to them during this silence, they laughed at me, or replied with clichés and well meaning ridicule. I did not find any soul mates with whom I could discuss *the collection of beautiful lights which wandered through my mind* during this silence in hostilities, and learned from then on out to refrain from any expectations of my fellows in combat to endure further speculation as to the mystical or meaningful nature of those lights

For some reason quite without sympathy from my army colleagues, I always though of the oft described two world wars as one long war with an interval. During the break, around about 1932, the second and concluding part of my experience occurred. Even though it was not possible to really be certain that the war begun in 1914 had not concluded in 1918 as popularly accepted, I lived in expectation of further action in Europe. As a professional army man then holding my final rank of Colonel, I was on leave from a dull stint in Palestine, and enjoying the peace and tranquillity which Broadwater Down was offering me. Such rare insight had been a quality undoubtedly bestowed upon my parents in their moving from London to the countryside. I was reaping the deferred rewards of their investment in my future. The house in which I dwelled was vast; to some an obscene waste of space, as I lived there quite alone, and without any desire to mate with a female, thus spawning fresh battle fodder for the continuance of the war.

One day, I looked out of my first floor bedroom window towards the house opposite, and without any hint of sexual intention, craned my neck to gain better sight of an older middle aged woman lying in bed; she would stare at the wall and then write down *perhaps* what she had seen. A man, maybe her husband, brought her a tray, and from it she poured tea, from the pot, into a delicate china cup. That she had purpose is without doubt, and her staring followed by scribbling was incessant for a long period, interrupted only by quick sips of tea. *The collection of beautiful lights wandered through my mind* for the second and last time, as the man who was perhaps her husband, closed the curtains on noticing my attention.

I recalled the futility of discussing this phenomenon I had now twice experienced, but made a childish mental note that should I reach the age of one hundred years old, I would record as accurately as is possible, the impact this experience had upon me. I say experience as a singular happening because I could not split one episode of it from the other, much as I always saw the two world wars as one.

I felt no desire to become better acquainted with these people who lived next door to me, yet knew that somehow we shared meaning of which perhaps we were not totally and utterly cognisant. A man calling himself Mr La Trobe-Bateman once apparently by mistake, knocked at my door apologetically asking about the lady living in the adjacent house; when I was unwilling to answer any of his superficially probing questions about the habits and aspirations of the occupants next door, he smiled knowingly and went on his way, but about which business I was unaware. I once stood next to that woman from the bedroom during a Sunday Church Service, but a mutual smile was all physically joining us that day, and I did not ever see her again. On the 16th December 1949, I lay gravely ill in the front room of my house, tended by a neighbour whose friend knocked to inform her that the lady who had lived next door all those years before, whom I had witnessed in her bed that day, had passed away the previous afternoon in the bed of a New York hospital. I smiled through my illness, and selfishly wondered if I was to join her, but it was not to be.

Now that the 30th June 1995 is well behind me, along with one hundred years of life, and I find myself a far lonelier figure amongst my own generation, I feel an urge and duty to write what will be perhaps my last useful act upon this earth for the time being. I happily recall the triangle of grass at the entrance to one end of Broadwater Down, with the typical red British telephone box standing proudly in the middle; the gout has won however, the cataracts occlude true physical vision and the scarce, unsubstantial food I am willing to eat, will probably enforce death upon me through malnutrition, and I am happy for it to so do.

Now to the meaning of these words ... I write of *connection* ... this word is all I can find to describe *the collection of beautiful lights which twice wandered through my simple mind in a single experience*. These lights made the war and myself as one; they gave meaning to the friends who had died all around me, sacrificing themselves needlessly for history, their King and their Country. The lights are life and life is those lights. They were as near to nothing as a human is able to contemplate ... and I forever recalled them whenever an opportunity arose, and by that I mean daily; it was only the aggregate of times per day I contemplated those lights which varied.

So my friends, I have recorded for posterity, the only experience I have ever had which has given meaning to my life. As you can imagine, it was not possible to successfully discuss it during life, and I am hopeful that it will take on greater meaning after it. To my friends who respectfully knew me as the brave soldier who has survived the great 1914 - 1945 war, it was an insignificant topic when compared to the great campaigns I undertook with gusto under the supervision of Field Marshall Montgomery. My magnanimous attitude and actions towards Indian independence was forever on their lips also, as well as that important corporeal question of practicality concerning just to whom I could bequeath the rambling mansion I inhabited, after my day of departure from this life.

I often think about the lady whom I witnessed in bed that day all those years ago, and wonder if she has ever thought about me; strange though, because it doesn't really matter either way. Now I wait, still contemplating my experience, with hope that *the collection of beautiful lights which twice wandered through my simple mind* will visit a third time, maybe lighting my way to a new bright life after this one has released me, for that event will not be long in coming.

> Colonel Harold Pendergrass Bradley died just after completing the story of his experience, which was found scribbled on a rough notepad which he left behind in his bedside cabinet; he bequeathed all his worldly possessions to a charity whose name nobody was able to discover ...

DEAR JOHN

> This note was written by John to himself, formed from an idea transmitted to him, which did not quite make it into one of his songs; rather, it formed the impetus which allowed an accurate flow of stimulation from wherever in particular he inspired it. It was discovered recently as part of a private collection owned by someone who wishes to remain anonymous. This wish is respected ...

14th December 1963

I have not written to you since your Mother died; as your Aunt allowed you a suitable upbringing for the life you wish to lead, I have seen little need to interfere. You are now famous and indeed show more talent than either of us expected. Your pains and patience from previous lifetimes is perhaps evident as gratification of a deferred nature.

Your songs are good, but say little that has not already been said before. Without a message, they still perform a service which is unique to the pop song genre, and enjoyed by millions as an escape from the hum drum existence they have allowed to form around their life potential. Next year in America, you will meet a poet songwriter, who will tell you physically what I am presently thinking your way in the ether.

Quite *what* you will say with the medium you have chosen, is the focus of my imminent meditations. If your *personality* is kept under control, and your *soul* qualities allowed to shine through, the impact you may have on world thinking could be *almost* unimaginable. This will be difficult however, as you have yet to firmly differentiate between these two qualities inherent within all physical consciousness.

The ideas that are accessible by incarnate humanity discriminate against none. All is available to all, and the sole arbiter of worth and ability to ingress the inspiration I and others outpour, lies within each individual. That you and I have particular rapport is because of an historical link through many millennia, and not the subject for this transmission.

So John, the next time we meet will be soul to soul, and I fear, sooner rather than later. Make the most of your world position for betterment of the mortal coil. Be kind to those your personality will inevitably discard along the way, and remember there is more to most than meets the eye.

I remain a loyal servant ...

Yours Sincerely,

JLGA

Fact And Inspiration

We were talking about the building of giant monuments, statues and pyramids all those years ago. All of the usual chit chat ensued, much as most of us have heard on Discovery Channel type programmes about The Easter Island Statues, and minority viewing programmes such as one I recall where contemporary man tried and failed to erect some massive stones, which according to our linear thought logic should be easier for us to manipulate now ... *now that we are modern that is!*

I mentioned my belief that these huge relics were built by 27 feet tall Atlanteans, who threw the stones around much as an apprentice chucks blocks to a brickie. The Storyteller, who also knew of this theory, preferred a recent explanation that the human form then was of similar dimensions to the present, but gravity was less dense when these buildings were erected, thus man was able to operate with far more vigour than are we, and was also capable of lifting much heavier weight. He described the land as being more spongy, less crystallised and easier to work, because of this lesser gravitational pull, and also because the earth was more infantile, which we can liken to a child's body, when compared to its parent's body which is older, harder and denser.

We talked of the moon's influence ... John said that without the moon and its tidal manipulation, water would not have receded, thereby allowing life to begin on land. I recalled the Rosicrucian viewpoint of how the moon was hurled from one of earth's oceans, and human lives which had not evolved thoroughly enough after that particular round of evolution, were sent to work out their destiny on that decaying crusty old ball of apparently negative influence. Poor things!

A cognition was forthcoming for me ... a self realisation which should help propel me on my way. *Contradicting data matters far less than the inspiration it provides!* We get hooked ever so easily on the accuracy of fact ... I remember eagerly awaiting a television programme about the search for Atlantis, which I could not even watch once to the end, it was so boringly filled with so much linear fact computed through these logical brains of ours, which we seem to access more and more, utilising less and less of their potential.

The cosmologies, and histories of the earth to which we have access, are certainly fascinating, and the information contained therein is frequently and dramatically inspirational. They all vary, and each has relevance to a different strain of humanity. *Many roads lead to Rome,* states the cliché, and nowhere more apparent than in the world of personal development. I encourage discussion about every aspect of life, but the minute a group or an individual becomes hooked on fact, it seems it or they lose some potential for inspiration.

If you find yourself faced with this choice, which way will you lean?

FROM RUSSIA WITH GRIEF

It was only a matter of time, before a suitable person would appear in connection with language translations for this body of personal development data which I have created over the years, and announce an interest. This had been visualised and planned; what had been omitted from any such blue print was a time scale, and when our newly discovered partner became involved in a Russian language translation of YOU CAN ALWAYS GET WHAT YOU WANT, called YOU CAN HAVE EVERYTHING YOU WANT, it was less than one month before the 1996 Frankfurt Bookfair, where we were to exhibit regardless of such a new relationship. It was obvious that it should be ready for this international event, if we were to maximise opportunities available through the attendance of so many buyers from Russian speaking countries.

When you have written a book which more or less describes the fact that most obstacles one encounters in life are self imposed, it is natural for readers of this material to expect super human qualities from the author; our new found partner, who only knew me through this mentioned book, quickly adjusted to my mortality, and it was soon apparent that we had equal amounts of something different to offer each other. His business outlook was fresh to our artistic approach, and vice-versa.

I am shocked in feeling an obligation to confess my initial faith in the ability of computer translation software packages to somehow delve into the depths of my psyche in order to drag from me accurate explanations to all I write. I thought this project would be quicker and easier than it turned out to be, and the lessons I learned from the venture became an important party of my inner personal development programme. It quickly became apparent that use of such software was inappropriate for all but the simplest of jobs ... *seeing the light* can be automatically translated into *looking at the lamp* ... *the path of personal development* could read *the road that you grew yourself* ... *consciousness, awareness, TTM, TFT, PAC, leader of the PAC, zipping, loadsamoney, a wedge on my hip, descriptions of the inner working of a mind,* all could illustrate a tendency for the computer to laugh at us by offering silly Russian phrases and words, which would mean the book ending up in the joke section of Moscow's large bookstores ... possibly and inadvertently making more money for us than if a more reliable translation job had been executed.

I began to visualise a telephone call from Stephen Pile, author of The Book Of Heroic Failures ... *Phil, we are compiling a new one called The Book Of Crap Translations; will you help us?* Joking aside, we had to find suitable translators quickly, and locally, if we were to meet the deadline. I felt that whoever we attracted would need some kind of grounding in Theosophy, or at least be an open hearted philosopher of ageless wisdom. Being a native of Russia was imperative, together with good word processing skills and hopefully a desire to form a long term relationship with myself and translation partner. Well, you know there are not that many people capable of such a job when you really have to find them. There was also the fact that the new partner was finding his way with us and quite naturally scrutinising the operation.

We found our people with the first telephone call made; when asked, they voiced an interest in forming a long term partnership and miraculously seemed to be experts in all that we sought. I was warned that in this day and age of post perestroika Glasnost, every Russian confessed to wizard status adeptness in everything, playing the trick of getting the job and then learning the necessary skill. So, our new found friends became bilingual touch typists of the translation variety, telling us how lucky we were to find them without having to endure other apparently less suitable people prospects.

Now, let us understand that the purpose of these words is not criticism of a mentioned party; they are written in an attempt to throw light on relationships, communications and interdependent difficulties between peoples of different cultures. Those who know me are aware that I have no interest in racism, sexism or indeed any other *ism* for that matter. Those same people may also be aware that I have no difficulty in both telling a so called *racist* or *sexist* joke, and being the butt of same. My only relevant interest would be in the purpose of such humour or standpoint. If it was to lift without any suffering, I would give it a mental tick; if it was to patronise or suppress, then a mental cross would be forthcoming.

Anyway, we all discovered together that computer translation software would not be suitable for the job. We agreed a price for the project, and spoke eagerly about the future. Our graphics designer and printer understood the urgency of the job, and its speculative nature; he offered us full use of his office, two AppleMac computers, and basically the facility to type right into the book format ready for film making.

The Russians were paid an amount up front, and then we noticed that they moaned often about most aspects of the job. *The deadline would not be achieved,* I was told, so I hastily rearranged all parties into another more suitable deadline ... as that one arrived, so did the demand for more money. With tears, criticisms and much melodrama, a market stall mentality was thrust upon me. We had already spontaneously offered them a further one quarter of our initial agreement, a fact which was little acknowledged, and now we were told more money was needed if the project was to continue.

I now confess a petty foible, and it is that if I am told to do something whilst the teller holds a gun to my head, I always shout *shoot!* Without a hope of finding replacements in time, I asked them to leave, with an accompanying explanation that under present behaviour patterns the whole deal had been blown by them, including the up until now not mentioned fact that we offered them money to accompany the project to Frankfurt, along with financial help to bring a friend of theirs from Moscow with a view to exploring interdependence with him also.

It is worth noting that these people were short of money at this time, yet occluded the fact with criticisms of our project, like announcing that we were paying them peanuts. I guess the clincher occurred when they demanded copyright of my book because of the work they had done for us in translating it into Russian. I risked a comparison between cultures; I asked if they were perhaps exhibiting Russian business manners in an English business environment, but I was asked to refrain from such nationalistic explanations.

They left and our friend who had lent us the office, computers, and so much of his time and expertise, showed us his true diplomatic worth by following them and consoling their grief at not getting what they wanted from the author of You Can Always Get What You Want, which by that time of course they had not only read, but assimilated all of the data before converting it into another language format.

> **Such assimilation of data does not go hand in hand however, with understanding and resultant wisdom!**

They returned, worked a continuous thirty six hour shift and readied the material for another hastily agreed deferred deadline. After a cycle of action lasting fifteen days, the book was transferred, close to midnight and zero hour, by modem, to the film makers, before it returned to us in film form for checking and despatch to the printing press.

My new Russian friends gave us over and above what anyone could expect from them. The work they produced is of a high quality; even though they moaned incessantly, constantly insisting that circumstances and conditions around them were just as they wished and not necessarily how others desired ... *no noise, no radio, no smoking.* There was still something special surfacing through that rash personality type behaviour however. We did not fall out, even though there was a lingering invitation to so do, and nor are we best friends. A cultural difference exists which we can either focus on as a problem, or celebrate as a challenge. *Vive la difference,* as French speakers say in the Ukraine.

We are in business, and safeguarded our threatened copyright in writing as a response to their demands. Their behaviour towards me resulted in the exact opposite of that which they desired to manifest. They wanted more money for the book but received exactly what had been agreed, plus our spontaneous bonus (offered before any disagreements surfaced). They indirectly accused us of exploitation in offering them what in fact was a generous amount of money plus accommodation to represent us in Frankfurt; we withdrew the offer and they got nothing. We offered assistance to their friend in Moscow, for him to meet us in Frankfurt to explore potential ... they wanted more so we cancelled the offer. They announced that they could earn more from teaching Russian as a language than they could working for us, and we promptly urged them to so do.

All methods that could have worked for them in Russia, worked against them in England. We would have gladly discussed any aspect of our financial relationship with them, but so long as there existed a hidden agenda, and they continued to ring others up to check on our reputation and the relationship of their fees to those of others working in bureaux, they got exactly what they had originally bargained for ... and not a rouble more or less.

Personal Development is about living the talk under the most extreme of circumstances and having your behaviour stand up to close scrutiny. The concepts we frequently discuss are easy to afford lip service, but it is to those out there in the real world of relationships and human interaction, who consistently grow with all they learn, that I doth my cap.

Real growth can only come from living and becoming a better, more able person through understanding ... no amounts of books or tapes in Russian or English will ever replace that experience!

Governments

There always seems to be someone somewhere, telling you what to do. They always know a better way of accomplishing a particular task, or a more effective way of communicating a certain sentiment. *That's not the way to do it ... this is the way to do it!* Products are advertised as being superior to their rivals, and personalities are heralded as being the real thing, when compared to a contemporary.

There are as many varying methods of government as there are willing and unwilling population recipients. Some are based upon the axioms of others, and have been changed just sufficiently, thereby allowing the country to which they apply, to call them their own. Others, proclaim themselves revolutionary and brand new.

My interest is in the metaphor. Analogous situations that benefit humanity are an easy way to communicate ideas and inspirations. A government is similar in nature to a Being in dominion over a personality and physical body.

The ultimate earthly government is The United Nations perhaps ... although there are some who would argue that the formation of such an organisation is a shield for world domination by a few powerful financiers ... so goes the conspiracy theory, although I must say The United Nations has the positive support of spiritually oriented groups whom I trust greatly. Then there are the governments representing nation groupings such as The European Parliament. The *first world* governments are all so called democracies, the *second world* governments almost so called democracies, and the *third world* governments still mainly stuck in a political time warp they must quickly mature from if they are to survive with live populations!

Throughout all of the foregoing descriptions, I sense similarities in these one people states we call human beings. We all utilise different types of government for our own ways of living. Some people still charge around like a third world dictator, dominating all within a sphere of influence, and condemning whatever disagrees with their one line thought system. I see democratic one people states dithering around trying to please some of the people some of the time, themselves mainly, and none of the people all of the time. I have watched second world personalities with their duplicitous ways, treading on all in their path *which is right,* but nobody being quite able to put a finger on just how they are doing it.

Basically and ultimately, we do not need governments at all; we do not need to think much really, and we certainly can survive without holding down any firm viewpoints. In fact, life is pretty much the opposite of how I viewed it as a reasoning and philosophising teenager, who knew all the answers and was willing to tell everyone just what they were. The more beliefs we create for ourselves, the longer it takes us to rid ourselves of them in order to progress and move onwards along the way. *But we need a belief in order to discard it and progress to the next,* I hear you think!

No we don't, I feel!

I recently wrote a letter to a Northern Irish Member of Parliament, and the Belfast Telegraph, saying the following ...

> We are not interested in any particular group in Northern Ireland; rather we are interested in all concerned achieving the honourable goal of peace. Prime movers in the instigation of such a situation in Northern Ireland are applauded by us, and of course you all have our positive thoughts for total success.
>
> It seems that experience is a quality one normally acquires just after it was most needed, but all concerned at this decisive hour in the history of Ireland, must

> make extraordinary efforts to utilise experience of a different nature ... an inherent experience born of compassion and desire for us all to live side by side in harmony. This can be accomplished, and we send out a clarion call for everyone to ponder this concept, for in doing so honestly, it is impossible for any of us to turn our backs on a bright new future of togetherness.

When a sense of universal good is available to you, beliefs are way behind what I describe as *an inherent experience born of compassion and desire for us all to live side by side in harmony.* Wars are born from beliefs; rifts created through the separating effects that beliefs must intrinsically have on their creators. Honestly, it is good to be harmless and easy to live successfully without a surrounding of beliefs.

Most of us think that we must consistently add to our skills and abilities if we are to personally develop. Well, sometimes it is better to discard than acquire. Beliefs fall into that category. The most difficult people to inspire are those who have become bigoted through their own beliefs. I often operate on the Internet, and I am rarely surprised to receive a communication beginning ... *I am a sceptic so don't think I'll be easy to convince* ... I never try; I usually endeavour to extricate myself honourably from any further connection for the time being, or, until the scepticism has worn itself out in life. *I know lots about this subject so I doubt you'll catch me* ... well, would I even bother; that certainly is not my role in life. *You'll never change my mind* ... defensive and assertive in one succinct phrase, but will the bearer of such a mind frame be capable of any useful progress during a lifetime?

A society is as criminal as it has numbers of laws to control that crime. Constantly emanated criticisms have the effect of pinning the criticism intended for others, to the criticiser ... you get kind of held in what wrestling would describe as *a half nelson hold,* until you release yourself from that criticism of others. Governments tie themselves to the crimes they are in fact desperately attempting to exterminate, by legislating against them ... the wheel turns and the cycles of action are repeated as we dig ourselves further into the mire with more laws, tighter regulations, stricter regimes, curfews, stronger punishments and harsher disciplines.

When you give attention to negativity, then and only then, does that negativity have power. Without your attention negativity cannot exist. Now this single piece of data is so powerful that it can change a person overnight from being a dithering one person state democracy, to a straightforward one person state looking for interdependent potential. The challenge then is to find other like minded people or organisations with few enough beliefs, laws and straight-jacket policies, with which to interdepend effectively.

You have the choice of government to employ for the rest of your lifetime and beyond. I invite you to ponder this inherent experience born of compassion and desire for us all to live side by side in harmony that we all have, in some hidden more effectively than in others. Ponder this concept, for in so doing honestly, it is impossible for any of us to turn our backs on a bright new future of togetherness.

Personal Development is fine ... but if you ended up as the only one developed there would be no other suitable humans with whom to interplay. It is together that we must evolve, and ending separateness whenever possible does wonders for the cause of mutual progress. Why else would a country like The United States, win a war by defeating Germany and Japan, then immediately begin helping them with policies like Marshall Aid, through which American money more or less rebuilt these two countries. Without them there would be no one with which to trade. Economies would collapse, chaos ensue and further wars become inevitable.

We must stabilise the world by making personal development

available to all. We must then suffer the egocentric turmoil created by those who discover the powerful new toys they call *mind power* and *will power,* and, *always being able to get what they want,* and, *communication tricks;* all independent and self-centred type behaviour is a natural step upward towards a more beneficial giving approach to life ... it goes onward and upward ever!

You can take a step right now by discarding your least useful belief!

GUARANTEES

What a fabulous age this is for the avid purchasers amongst us who enjoy consumer durables, and the consequent workload they ease from this mortal coil. *Caveat Emptor* was the phrase which provoked fear into the very soul of our ancestors who dared contemplate the purchase of anything, from coal to coat hangers. For those of us unlucky enough to miss out on the advantages of the Latin language in our basic education, of which I was one, this phrase means *buyer beware.* In other words, once an item had been purchased, the responsibility for its efficacious potential became the customer's.

Only relatively recent has change to this modus operandi occurred; now altered significantly in the purchaser's favour. *Caveat Venditor* is my description of a new cry heard from the marketplace; it means *seller beware.* Vendors now suffer an almost total responsibility for every aspect of the sale in which they engage, from the description of goods in an advertisement, to the delivery, unpacking by the buyer, and often, the capabilities of customers in the usage of a particular item.

Try it free for a month and see how you like it, I regularly read; *satisfaction guaranteed or your money back,* is another significant yield to the customer; *if it is not what you want, just return it in its original packaging for a full refund,* is my final example.

The faith placed in the hands of purchasers is now extreme, and as ever, the minority are present to illude that trust as misplaced. The words you are presently reading, were composed utilising a computer and software purchased mail order via a computer magazine, during a time period when prices were steadily declining, and specifications were healthily rising. Two weeks after the system had arrived and was running smoothly, with a degree of customisation attended to, the following month's magazine dropped through the letterbox to announce a price reduction of £300, and an increased specification to the CD ROM and hard drives. I was right in the middle of a thirty day agreement which would have allowed me to return the items, only to purchase them again at a price and specification advantage. I had deliberately bought the computer system as a limited guard against the built in obsolescence suffered with my previous combination, and here within two weeks I was faced with slower, weaker and more expensive equipment than I would have liked.

Well, I kept the system as originally purchased, after accepting that I had willingly bought goods which arrived exactly as described in the advertisement, and it was none of my business that the company found it necessary to make adjustments to the deal similar to that agreed with me. End of story, until I was reminded of the episode yet again the following month when the price dropped another two hundred pounds ... I found myself counting the depreciative cost of this system by the week!

Those who would return the goods under similar circumstances, perhaps under the banner of, *as agreed, legally correct, they said it was okay to, the contract stated* ... are in fact guilty of trusting moral rights and obligations within themselves, to the small print contained within a purchase agreement composed by another. I know almost all of the justifications for a selfish attitude in cases such as that described, and they are invariably good superficially and bad ultimately. In fact eventually, any violation of such a trusting commercial procedure will rebound onto an individual with the exact same force enjoyed initially by that person in the execution of the abuse.

There are many instances of such situations in which you may find yourself leaning towards an infringement of this new found trust in mercantile procedures; *taking a dress back to Marks and Spencer after accidentally ripping the material, utilising any guarantee for your own ends when the vendor is not at fault, demanding much more than honestly necessary on an insurance claim, taking advantage of bureaucratic errors, not placing money in honesty boxes, failing to tax a car, not paying a parking fine, ignoring genuine requests to clarify erroneous situations which have occurred to your advantage* ... this list could grow very long!

If we fail to recognise just how fortunate western populations are, we may find ourselves hurtling back through space and time into the dark ages still endured by many second and third world populations, as they struggle to buy and sell their way through life by swimming with the sharks and frequently being eaten by them.

The actual impulse to include the title GUARANTEES with this book, occurred whilst I was pondering the purchase of a language translation software package at my local computer store. The assistant suggested that I buy it, install the programmes on my computer, then return it for a full refund, and I would have just what I wanted ... and certainly not what his employers would desire! Of course this episode made me think about the general ambience of such dealings, and what you read here is pretty much what I have concluded. For the record, I did not do as this superficially friendly chap had suggested, but grant that his criminal proposition had a positive side to it as stimulation for this preventative material to be written.

I have been offered personal development audio programmes to duplicate onto cassette, and when mentioning the infringement of copyright this would entail, accusations of softness and stupidity have been uttered. Yet those same people who criticise individual viewpoints as mine is on this issue, will shout to be heard at the disgusting attitude to copyright infringements the Russians and Chinese have as a nation. Likewise, they would threaten County Court action should those same people be faced with *a shoe on the other foot!*

A person cannot do right in one department whilst attempting to do wrong in another, said Mahatma Gandhi quite rightly. If you try, whatever is engaged will be but a pale imitation of its true potential. The crucial challenge we face when encountering similar situations to those described in this bite, is actual honesty within our own universe. Owning up to the rightness of a decision as a spiritual being, whilst being threatened by the lower self with an allegation of idiocy.

The significant problems we face cannot be solved at the same level of thinking we were at when we created them, stated Albert Einstein, but how many of us are willing to *up the anti* on the thought stakes, when faced with short term gain at long term cost!

I witnessed a father dupe the vendor of a water jet ski machine into allowing himself and three others from his family, a long and entertaining demonstration of the vehicle for the purpose of determining if purchase would occur. With no plan to buy, and a direct intention to deceive, this was a lesson to the youngsters in the art of fraud, whilst whizzing around The English Channel for free, at someone else's expense. That is not clever, it is *so* easy! The challenging attitude is to *not* do that type of thing. Yet most of us succumb to the pull of our lower selves, and as we so do, add a piece of negativity to the process of evolution, which is really there to be enjoyed.

It is easy to fool the dog into thinking you have thrown a stick, when it in fact still remains in the hand behind your back. Children can be duped regularly with similar schemes time and time again, often to the delight of adults choking on the strains of hilarity as it is rendered audible.

When you reach a certain plateau of development, *as spirit having a human experience,* the only guarantee worth possessing is available from yourself. This also means that at times, it is necessary to insist on personally beneficial action even when no guarantee has been offered by another. It is only when you have assumed total responsibility for every little facet of your existence, will niggly little bothersome incidents cease to impinge on your life. When they cease to be effectual, the larger ones can then be confronted. As long as you mooch around the insignificance of small minded worlds, you will have your head facing down over in full view of the gutter.

As you rid yourself of increased dollops containing self serving episodes stimulated by mind numbing and soulless lack of creative thought, you may notice your head rising in its elevation, until eventually it is able to contemplate the horizon, to some which is new every time it is pondered, and to others, still there after all this time.

Give yourself a challenge, be self insured and personally guaranteed, contemplate new horizons with each day dawning, celebrate civil and human rights wherever they are demonstrated, and live the talk espoused by your higher self; for in these upper echelons of your life, here and only here, is where you may experience *the real you,* as the lower personality illusion side of you waits in distracting obedience for your attention once again. The opportunity is then repeated.

I guarantee that as a fact of life!

GURUS

In Hinduism, a guru is a spiritual teacher. The word originally would have been *guruh*, from the Sanskrit language, and initially meant *heavy* or *venerable*. We frequently utilise the word colloquially, to mean simply, *a charismatic leader or guide*. I often hear people describing a particular mentor as their guru. This outlook is now thoroughly westernised, and it is not uncommon to find many personal development teachers and authors endowed with this title.

It is a fact in Personal Development, that eventually a pupil will usually tire of the teacher. This occurrence is scarcer in religion however, where it is quite uncommon to find someone who really admired Jesus Christ, suddenly going off him. How rare is it to hear a Buddhist describing his disillusionment with Gautama Siddhartha Buddha, or a Hindu criticising Brahma, Vishnu or Shiva. Many do however, confuse these people with the organisations others have thrown around their original teachings and decide to not like these religions.

The point to bear in mind, is that sentiments often described and encouraged by more ancient teachers, is usually of an ageless nature, and the tricks mainly disseminated in the Personal Development industry are mostly fashionable and hip. There is a trend as I write these words, for western minds to lean eastwards, and allow previously untried outlooks to permeate their universe. This is an excellent step forward, unless it is taken hoping for a total personality based transformation to occur before the morrow has dawned!

During our onward momentum, and in true esoteric tradition, all outlooks should be investigated, along with a diversity of knowledge and a variety of methods for attaining one's goals. Putting on the saffron robes does not maketh the man however, and a trip down to the local new age emporium does not guarantee nirvana as the after life. Nor does choosing a guru and expecting that through the connection with this personality alone, sudden meaningful and everlasting transformations will be forthcoming.

Any so called guru that leaves you with a sense of reliance upon him or her, or a feeling that to absent yourself from an onward connection will prove disastrous ... is not a guru. Real teachers are those who pray that their pupils will eventually overtake them, to have the teacher-pupil relationship reversed. If it is not this way then some kind of personality based equation has interrupted the true beauty of providing inspiration as a guru.

I know of one organisation which has no process in its rules and regulations that allows a person once enrolled, to *route off* from a connection with the establishment. In fact, when a person tries to accomplish an honourable retreat from such dependence, they are told that they must have misunderstandings about the technology they have been learning, and are urged to pay for another process which will help reveal what their error of judgement has been. Good old fashioned brainwashing still rearing its head as the 21st century dawns eh!

I do not know of one case, where continued reliance on a guru was encouraged by any real teacher of ageless wisdom. The great names which spring to mind are Krishnamurti, H P Blavatsky, Alice Bailey, Jesus Christ, Buddha and Krishna, but there are many more, as you may know. It seems that the wiser, greater and more ageless is the teaching, the less one feels inclined away from it. In other words, truth is everlasting, and not to be confused with fads and fashions.

Now, all that is possible within confines of the modern definition of personal development, is a diluted version of that great body of knowledge which we know as The Ageless Wisdom. In its purest form, it is not palatable for everyone immediately, and so, personal development teachers rear their heads and talk of magic ways to always get what you want from life, and describe their work as empowering whilst encouraging you to take a number of steps, all the time remembering that before every beginning is a thought.

In line with the teachings of Krishnamurti, I honestly believe that ...

> **... all beliefs are mental and spiritual straight-jackets. All religions are a convenient way to offload personal responsibility and the only way to freedom and enlightenment is through self observation. The only challenge we really have is getting down to the business of doing it!**

A guru who does anything but present certain basic truths for your assimilation and experience, is not performing a valid role. The only way forward is by medium of spontaneous self cognition, and for this to occur you need only the most basic of tools ... yourself!

It is not everyone who can face this fundamental axiom with ease however. We are used to dressing up truth in fancy clothes and endowing universal laws with names that immediately negate any usefulness the knowledge of them would have had for us on our route to increased awareness. So, the personal development industry steps in and people like me write about human potential and universal evolution.

My biggest aspiration is that Phil Murray books and tapes will be irrelevant in the not too distant future, because of their elementary content. My work is a mere stepping stone to the vast body of unlimited potential which lies within each of us ... frequently dormant in the main, but stating its case with greater force and frequency as each decade passes. You do not need to read and study anything, and no lectures are prerequisites, to realise what you have available for free any time of day during every day of the week. You just have to get down to the job in hand.

For you, the most powerful guru in this universe *is* you!

HAPPINESS

I recently contributed to a BBC Radio programme, and was asked to talk about WHAT MAKES LIFE WORTH LIVING. My initial response was to flippantly declare that contemplation of the alternative would seem to impel most of us along the conscious line, rather than choosing the unconscious option. Yet, to me death *is* the great adventure, to paraphrase an Alice Bailey title, and certainly not what makes life worth living. Many of my contemporaries believe that one has not lived until death has been experienced, and this would indeed correspond with my own feelings on the subject.

This line of thought however, would not have been suitable for the discussion forum in which I was to partake; I therefore approached the subject from a different angle. In doing so, my contemplations were drawn time and time again to the American Pledge which describes the *pursuit of happiness* being a right of all human beings, along with *life and liberty*.

The pursuit of happiness was in fact my conclusion to the question asked of me. The words must be contemplated however, and in doing so you may find many varying facets to the concept. If you have ever tried just being happy, you will know that it is very difficult, until you cease treating happiness as an emotion, and begin to accept the senior harmonic of serenity as a more worthy goal, that is.

Happiness occurs during the accomplishment of an otherwise unrelated goal, I wrote in YOU CAN ALWAYS GET WHAT YOU WANT, and it is these exact words which convey my feelings on this question. You must be active with some onward momentum connected to your purpose, for happiness to be forthcoming as a *by-product* of that momentum. Much like inflowing money is a *by-product* of executing some kind of service for others, so too with happiness.

The senior harmonic of happiness I mentioned as serenity, and this can be a target during periods of stillness, which we call meditation, TTM, (the acronym for Time To Myself) or whatever name you may feel is relevant. The more serenity you achieve, the less happiness you will seek; the less happiness you seek, the happier you will become; the more serene you are will equal your magnetic capabilities to attract the good which is all around you.

All is interwoven with all. It is not possible to separate any aspect of life from another without creating further illusion, and we have enough of that on earth already. I believe in balance, and I always suggest that a combination of personality oriented goals with spiritual aspiration will harbour within that relationship the seeds of true accomplishment. Happiness will be forthcoming, and if you are on the right track, serenity will lie alongside it.

I wish you both ...

HONESTY

This first observation occurred in 1978, whilst I was signed to the most important recording contract I ever had during my years in the music business. One evening a few of us were shooting the breeze at our manager's house, when the Mescal bottle was brought out for inspection ... the one with the dead worm floating in it. None of us had dared imbibe this Mexican drink, and consequently it had remained in place whilst countless Bacardi bottles had passed it by on the shelf, serving us well. This was a long time ago!

The manager offered £1.00 for each shot of Mescal successfully swallowed and held down. As you may gather we had plenty of time on our hands to engage in such trivial pursuits. I drank twelve shots, pocketed the £12.00, and could barely focus my eyes. However, we were all in much the same state of inebriation, but between the giggles and secular social intercourse, my manager offered a further challenge. He suggested that as I had worked in the music business all of my life, I would be unable to obtain gainful employment elsewhere, and were I to prove him wrong by obtaining a musically unrelated job the very next day and retaining it for a minimum of one month, he would donate a further £100.00 to my overdrawn bank account.

The next day, with head swimming in an alcoholic hangover, I obtained an immediate interview for the position of security officer, this title describing a job for which few questions were to be asked, with a local company connected to the print industry. I was successful and started this gainful employment the following day. After a month £100.00 duly appeared in my account together with my first month's wages. The overdraft which had been in place for two years by that time, had showed few signs of decreasing, and had prompted more than a few impersonal and unkind letters from transient managers and assistants who found music business circumstances difficult to comprehend, and lack of a regular monthly salary impossible to tolerate. I fended off the attacks on my financial credibility, but was now confronted with a chance to repay this money within six months.

I decided to stay. The record contract was still in place, and the shifts which I worked allowed me to continue my musical progress unabated, although a little more tired than usual when working the night shift. During the second month, I decided that if I was to stay for a total of six months, I should at least be an *excellent* security officer. I had begun my studies of philosophy and spirituality four years earlier, and the main lesson that I had learned was connected to ethics and morals; I consequently felt well capable, although in actual fact over qualified, to protect the well being of this company that was enhancing my financial status.

There were eight officers in addition to myself, all of whom tolerated me whilst my intentions towards the company were transient, but when told of my new plan to stay, bar one, found it difficult to contain their intolerance and suspicion of me. *Methinks he doth protest too much,* was a Shakespearean quote which often came to mind whenever I touched on a question to colleagues concerning honesty, and that infinite question of right and wrong. Before the old chief security officer retired, he took myself and another of the eight with whom I am still friends after all this time, into an infrequently visited part of the factory, and introduced us to some items which were favourites for theft and subsequent profit ... by security officers. It seems our apprenticeship had been served and the goodies were now available, to spite the other seven officers whose parting gift this was from the retiring c.s.o.

During the first week of power for the new c.s.o., I reported someone leaving the factory with enough copper tube to install a central heating system into an average detached house; I was told to let it pass. My friend, disillusioned with opportunities in England, returned to Germany where he had formerly served in the armed forces as a musician for many years. I was alone, and it became apparent that my personal honesty was threatening colleagues. I believe this to be the single most significant challenge we all must face when changing paradigms in our lives for the better; such changes do not necessarily feel instantly good for those around us.

Many wheezes were utilised to get rid of me, and the final one worked, coincidentally after six months, just as my clinging overdraft was repaid and my music schedule was becoming busier. The company made us all redundant and re-employed all except me. I must have posed some threat for such negative influence to be employed in their ridding themselves of the only truly honest one amongst them. This was an important step in my own learning process, but one which I appreciate far more in retrospect than whilst experiencing it at the time!

A few years later, after the collapse of an American recording contract which had seen me staying in Beverley Hills and the Hollywood Hills, I returned to England, midwinter, with yet again very little money, lots of experience and a hankering for the exploration of avenues beyond the narrow confines of music biz land. I got myself an acting agent, who promptly sent me for an audition which I passed, and off I went on a major theatrical tour for the remainder of that winter. I returned much the wiser, and eminently more qualified for more advanced acting work. The same production company sent me on another main theatre tour the following year, for six months. I shared a dressing room with a 16 year old actor who played my son in the production. He was fresh out of drama school, good fun, but not yet rid of that schoolboy mentality that has little room for sentiment, the feelings of others, or in fact anything that does not have *self* printed all over it.

During the second week of that tour, he reported to the company manager that £10.00 had been stolen from his pocket during a time period when it would only have been possible for it to have been stolen by me! This sounds petty does it not? You must visualise the small minded, narrow and secular world of a group of actors touring the country, who have lots of time to spend apart from their work. Gossip and rumour are often chosen by such companies in preference to creativity and endeavour. This accusation to say the least was devastating, as, much like an accusation of rape, even when found innocent, one still remains tarred by the blaming brush!

Now this episode was all the harder to tolerate for me as I had undertaken a personal oath of honesty, integrity and truth in all with which I was involved. It was therefore curious that it should be me who attracted this negative vibration. I refuted the accusation and the matter was left in stalemate. I observed the accusing colleague closely over the following days, and in fact deliberately became quite matey with him; at times we shared hotel bedrooms, imbibing occasional after show drinks together. It was during one such extended imbibing session that he showed me some stolen credit cards which he had purchased the previous Sunday from a friend whilst visiting home. I laughed when he offered to sell me one, and by this time I was plainly safe for him to be with, to the degree that he volunteered his mistake in accusing me earlier of that theft ... *the tenner had showed up,* he confessed.

I watched and listened to that young whippersnapper throughout the remainder of the tour, and pieced together just what his game was. His background lay in that murky crossover world between the criminal and not too criminal life. His game relevant to me was to place suspicion firmly with someone else at the beginning of that tour, so that he could steal as the opportunity arose, without ever attracting the uncomfortable stare of accusatory eyes. It was a cold and ruthless way of being for one so young, and rendered all the more effective by his likeable image and ample acting capabilities.

Honesty is a way of life. Most honest people are only relatively honest and not necessarily honest by default. The majority are easily swayed across the criminal line, and few treat honesty integrally with their personal philosophy, worthy of exploration as part of a way towards living a more effective life. Honesty is not just connected with *to thieve or not to thieve!* When you decide on honesty as part of your personal philosophy, it becomes apparent that every single aspect of your life must be touched by it. There is an obligation for instance, to honestly convey as a third party, communications as they are intended rather than interpreted. Honesty must be accepted in the thought world. You must be spiritually honest, and not claim status not rightly yours! You may no longer make life easier for yourself by communicating what others wish to hear rather than what you need to convey.

I need write no more on this subject, as it will become apparent to those who honestly choose the honest route, all that I am able to convey plus more, and such understanding will be far more effective as a personal cognition, than anything I am able to write relevant to your life.

I invite you to be honest ... the mere decision is all that is needed to get you started; such determination however, is but the beginning of the constant challenges which life will throw your way in an effort to have its random way with you.

Good luck!

HUMANIMAL

There is no doubt whatsoever, in any corner of my evolving universe, that the apparent twin aspects of spirit and animal within humanity, make life both hard to live, and paradoxically so, worth living. The genesis of our human form is a fascinating subject itself, and a mixture of information taken from Madame Blavatsky's Secret Doctrine, Max Heindel's Rosicrucian Cosmo-Conception, most religions and The Urantia Book, helps many of us to formulate an intuitive sense of corporeal history. What we do with such awareness is the subject of this bite.

We seem to live in an age where evolutionary balance exists, between the animal side and the spiritual potential of humanity. Most of us could therefore be deemed HUMANIMALS. There are those who lag behind, and some who are way out in front; the possible combinations of attributes each of us are able to manifest defies description. We can have terrific mental capacity and little compassion; all love and no brain; physically strong and intelligently weak; ugly bodies and beautiful insides; creative fingers and dumb toes; intuitive spiritually and incomprehensible in relationships ... with all of the grey areas between these dichotomies in which most of us may be caught lurking!

Ever the object of my personal development brand is balance ... learning to celebrate all potential which exists for us to utilise. Consequently, it is beneficial for us all to spend time exploring areas of weakness for the purpose of repair, rejuvenation, development or just plain interest. In this logical world of evolving mental capacity, where kudos is afforded those with intellect, physical strength and capacity to be devious, it therefore falls on most of us to explore the heart aspect of living with compassion.

If you have ever tried exploring this subject with a person heavily socialised into the rational guise of all things logical being visible, all can be taught with text books, big thick heavy manuals are essential and compassion for a rival is a sign of softness, you may know what a seemingly uphill task this is. Yet, up until this approximate time, as it has been humanity's capacity to evolve beyond the potential of our animal cousins utilising chiefly our grander mental capacity, so too is it now our task to evolve beyond this mental prowess into the realms of heart capabilities.

It is this heart area I describe which really sets us apart from the animal kingdom. We are able to exhibit charity, justice and generosity; in fact these qualities are bursting to be seen in most of us. It is through real personal development that animal becomes humanimal becomes human, before eventually transcending this bite into another not relevant for this book. It is material wrapped in the insignia of personal development which teaches tricks and trivia about the way we are and can be, yet the result is remaining the same with a few added gimmicks, that is the worst antagonist to a truer understanding of what indeed we actually are.

We have organisations like MENSA formulated for those with a high intelligent quotient, who utilise narrow criteria to judge the worth of an individual for membership. It is my experience that a high IQ has little relating it to the worth of an individual in connection with both society and that individual. If you have ever been in a room populated by a segregation of such people, you may agree with me just how uninspiring those circumstances can be. Yet a sprinkling of heart oriented humanity within such confines can transform that atmosphere. As is this interpersonal scenario, so it is within an individual's own personal universe. Diversification is necessary to balance the heart and head aspect of us all, and as I have already intimated, for most of us this means casting attention onto our love potential.

Fairly well known Latin phrases like *mens sana in corpore sano,* means, *a sound mind in a sound body*, usually suggesting that mental well being is dependent on physical well being. May I add to this equation that I believe physical well being to be dependent on one's ability and inclination to outflow charity, justice and understanding, perhaps under the generic description of love. Head freaks may well be intelligent, but only a fraction of their potential aptitude is possible, until love is contemplated and implemented as the one true capacity we are all able to utilise as a panacea.

Maybe we need a metaphorical heart organisation to run alongside MENSA which we can call CORSA, formed from the Latin *cor,* meaning heart, and equally ambiguous as is its mental equivalent, at judging the worth of an individual. Yet, the two words from which our two organisation's names are derived, seem to almost mean the same thing much of the time, depending on their Latin context. It seems that both can mean *judgement,* and this word describes the real attribute available to us when a balance of head and heart is utilised. *Lack of good judgement* is apparent when an imbalance is present.

Calibrate your twin assets, is the message contained within these words. *Regulate* any imbalance by paying closer attention to the least present. *Tune* your human engine which contains a carburettor called a brain, and a pump called the heart. Too much of one leads to lack of economy and an absence of speed; in this state you will get nowhere fast, which is what happens to many people when they home in on the personal development gimmicks endemic in most *How To* books, also visible in underdeveloped work leaning heavily on past success formulae designed for bygone generations.

Humanimals must now initiate themselves into the realms designed for humanity, by revealing qualities presently impossible in less evolved species; I have already mentioned some ... charity, justice and understanding ... contemplate these concepts and their use, and if you sense that practical manifestation of them represents a portion of humanity's fate, then serve us all by brandishing them in an outpouring of love.

IN WHAT SHOULD WE ALL BELIEVE

Nothing and everything; all and sundry; forever and a day; you and me! Beliefs are not going to disappear overnight, yet as it become increasingly obvious that they are ill equipped to serve us beyond the level of thinking at which we currently find ourselves, it would be wise for the cognoscenti amongst us to contrive a strategy for escaping their lair at an early opportunity.

Some of us are still entrapped by the organised religions which have emerged over the millennia to dominate our thought limitations; yet, if you demolish all of the churches, synagogues, temples, chapels, abbeys, cathedrals, basilicas, mosques and chantrys, the collective divinity of which we are all part, often called God, still exists. Do we have to be seen going to church in order to be judged how good we are, or can we just allow a reflection of what is inside us to radiate this description?

Just as a variety of churches emerged to attempt the teachings of some of the great who have exemplified distinguished human incarnation, so too does a variety of individual beliefs exist to help us live life with greater understanding. I have no desire to unload yet more beliefs onto a society positively groaning under the weight of such contrivances, but this is indeed a challenge, to avoid passing on mental maps which ultimately you will have to discard anyway.

Celebrating the differences and learning from other approaches, I always find an invigorating experience, so if we have to endure beliefs, why not at least believe in a refreshed belief of fellow humanity; perhaps this is one more step towards a life of absent opinion about anything. What I am presenting for public scrutiny is an idea which forms the base for most religions, yet is rarely affirmed, which we can describe as *granting beingness*. To describe this ancient idea further, it would include allowing others to be themselves just as you strive to be more you yourself! Turning the other cheek, would be a sympathetic sentiment, hopefully never needing to be used, and live and let live is another appropriate motto.

The thing is that we so rarely instigate these ideas into relevant episodes of life. It is so much easier to just have the belief, than it is to slam that belief into action. The moment any of our basic fears enter the equation, most of us reach for the handiest belief to aid our navigation through the valley of death! Fears of poverty, criticism, ill health, loss of love, old age, loss of liberty and death, are what Napoleon Hill equates as our seven basic fears; he further urges that *since fear is merely a state of mind, you can control it by taking action.*

With the reigns once more in my hands, I suggest that as fear is a state of mind on which most of the world's organised religions prey, it is folly to combat fear by remaining within the mental universe through merely creating or reinforcing more beliefs, like positive affirmations of the negative fear! Give yourself a practical exercise to illustrate this idea I am postulating. Recall your strongest belief and then change your mind about it ... cease to believe in it ... are you still alive? Of course you are! Just like God surviving the burning of the temples, every human being has the innate capacity to exist without anything else but existence!

Knowing this data, should aid any individual assault on success in every single aspect of any life. In order to reach the real you, just like peeling an onion, you have to strip the layers of beliefs you have accumulated, to discover that bright light more powerful than any laser, which is the divine spark known as you. By all means believe in yourself, but you do not have to. Even whilst believing in yourself, the knowledge that you do not have to, makes that believing less stressful. Believe in others if you will, but they can have fulfilled lives without any belief oriented attention from you. *Grant beingness,* is my urge; celebrate the difference; learn from the variety; enjoy the contrast and allow the contrariety to educate.

...

A latecomer to the PAC one evening, sat nervously awaiting the first possible window into the conversation, for the purpose of inculcating us with his viewpoint, which more or less followed the premise that everything we uttered had already been realised by him in a far simpler format, which he described to us utilising clichés and toupés and threepés, to quote the old 10cc song called Silly Love. His belief system had altered enough to permit him entry into the world of personal development and self improvement, but it would only allow progress at a certain speed and up to a specific point. We had travelled beyond, which made him uncomfortable, reaching for his nearest belief, which in this case was that *everything does not have to be as complicated as we were making it.*

Frequently the case; I agreed with him, before exploring even deeper that topic with which we were engaged, trying not to tread on his surrounding and suffocating beliefs! Many years ago, the group with which we evolved would discuss whether or not there existed one trigger, which, when pulled, would catapult a person into self realisation. *Death with a continuity of consciousness* was the only useful answer to which I was attracted; yet, I feel that more than twenty years later, we are discussing that same topic again, albeit from a slightly different perspective.

Avoiding beliefs, ridding yourself of belief accumulation and not going into agreement with already existent beliefs, may be that trigger we postulated all those years ago. A surge of trapped energy is unleashed with each belief ceased. If you are to engage in this process of *stripping the crap,* you may then utilise the released energy for good purpose, perhaps initially to trigger the discharge of another belief. As we are able to think about how we think, this almost places us under an obligation to so do. It is however, an ability latent within us all, yet utilised presently by the few.

Are you one of the few? Can you aspire towards a cessation of beliefs? Will you think about how you think and improve the quality of those contemplations?

You can if you want!

JESUS CHRIST AND THE CHRISTIANS

What a man; what a mission; what an example; what a religion; what a mess! *Because a man prays long and loud is not a sign that he is a saint,* wrote Levi in *The Aquarian Gospel Of Jesus the Christ.* Likewise, *because a person says that he is into Alice Bailey, Max Heindel, Anthony Robbins, Brian Tracy, Wayne This and Shakti That, A Course in Mirages and How To Lose Enemies and Incapacitate People,* writes Phil Murray in his fifth personal development book, *is not a sign that they are any better than they were before!*

It is a signal from some that change may be imminent, but from others, merely a way of influencing how you see them. I remember proudly announcing to an acquaintance in my younger years, that I had just purchased a stereo Sony television set ... when they were rare. He smiled, as he replied that he was *just about to purchase* a superior model. That was his power, or so he thought. He did not ever, to my knowledge, make such a purchase, or even one that resembled it for our purposes. He just wanted to look good and put me down a notch or two. That was his long, loud prayer!

I live in the general vicinity of many varying philosophical organisations. Some set themselves up against each other, whilst others quietly inter-snipe at the least opportunity. I wrote the following words for an early Positive Attitude Club Newsletter ...

> A joy of living in this particular southerly area of the United Kingdom, is the fact that so many different philosophically based organisations have set up either headquarters or branches here. I have heard many explanations for this phenomenon, including the possibility that our location is apparently at a high energy intersection of lay lines. There is also the physically pragmatic aspect of being close to London, whilst retaining the advantages of country life.

> I often stand at a certain point on the Ashdown Forest where I can see the North Downs, which are my buffer against the hustle-bustle of the city, and the South Downs, which represent to me, a protection from the sea, and when I do this it gives me a feeling of privilege.
>
> Whether or not we disagree with the creeds or philosophies of any of these organisations with which we share space, is irrelevant compared to the uniqueness of each individual energy type made available to us all, through them.
>
> Refuse to speak disparagingly of any ... focus on the qualities of each ... and remember that the PAC is totally and utterly independent ... our policy is interdependence!

Even though most people who know me understand my viewpoint on criticism, I am still frequently asked for an opinion about organisations which overlap onto my sphere of influence ... Mormons, Theosophists, Pagans, Christian Science, Scientology, Masonry, Rudolph Steiner's Educational Establishments ... the list could continue!

The Scientology Headquarters are at Saint Hill Green, which is near East Grinstead, West Sussex, and this ensures a regular supply of questions from opponents of this cult, to me, about their validity as a way of developing as spiritual beings. If you want to know about Scientology, study Scientologists, would perhaps be a good recommendation in this instance. However, it came to my attention when someone told me that L Ron Hubbard, the deceased founder of this sect, states quite categorically that Scientologists are not Scientology. What is it then, if one is unable to at least in part, judge the material by its results with fellow humanity at which it is aimed? Is this the simplest and most cynical disclaimer ever invented?

I understand that there may be more to any given subject than the sum of the knowledge any one individual retrieves from the greater store, but I am afraid that there is no other way of judging any group other than by the examples it creates within society. If you want to be one of those examples then go ahead and jump right in ... sample for yourself ... but the chances of you ending up far different from any other example thus far created by any philosophical foundation, is virtually nil!

In the case of Scientology judging for yourself would mean completing a course, having some of what they describe as auditing, or even perhaps signing a one billion year contract to become a member of what they call the Sea Organisation. Money is invariably involved, and inevitably the flow is mainly from you to them.

Through the years, being a Christian has involved killing of other Christians because they don't understand Christianity as you do; being a Mason has included keeping from the masses and even ordinary Masons, the true and honourable purpose of Masonry; the Mormons record the names of every person who has been privileged to roam this earth ... even though to my line of thought this means recording the same spiritual beings time and time again in their various human guises, as well as new ones; the Steinerites protect an excellent educational philosophy which is now out of date by the very fact that it was written in an age where modern times could not have been accurately visualised; adherents to the undoubted wisdom of the Alice Bailey books must suffer a stifling of any individual onward inspiration if they connect up with the Trust established to keep her books in print and the philosophy available ... illustrated by an unwillingness to have the words of *The Great Invocation* adapted to suit modern non sexist viewpoints, and not mine I might add.

Now, Jesus was one of the greatest people to incarnate for an earthly existence, acting as an agent for the Christ energy to be demonstrated on earth, but without doubt he and this energy must karmically answer for the result of his teachings ... a mass of twisted interpretations of his messages exist at variance with even themselves sometimes. Of course, this may well have been part of the lesson, but I believe that the time has come to clean up the mess and *Onward Christian Disarmed Soldiers Go!*

If you want to find Christ, Buddha, Jesus, Jesus The Christ; *the truth* of Scientology, Mormonism, Christian Science, Theosophy, The Alice Bailey Philosophy ... *by its own admission,* et al, they are in the self same easily accessible private palace inside your very own universe.

Christ is in you, me, and the wall!

Because the words of any member of humanity are worthless unless they translate into actions which enhance the evolution of humanity onward and upward ever, it is sad to reflect on any that do not inspire your world within, and consequently your world without, which you share with the rest of us. Don't pray long and loud so that someone will see you; do it because you will hear yourself inside and translate your desires into a better world. You! God! Christ! Buddha! Call it what you will, and if it makes a difference to an expansion of our collective consciousness then I will agree with you.

The words do not matter nearly so much as the sentiment behind them and the impulse which drives the words forward into goodwill. I invite you to get armed with enough knowledge to fuel your own sensing of the future ... as long as it is a better future for all. Call yourself what you will, but you will discover as you progress along this interesting way forward which we call *The Path,* that the name is always secondary to the nature!

LETTER FROM AMERICA
written in Clearwater, Florida

Here we are again ... each time we holiday, or live, in our favourite part of the States, new realisations dawn. Not faster or greater than those we could ordinarily expect were we to remain in England forever, just environmentally stimulated.

We can switch on the television and watch Deepak Chopra deliver his *seven spiritual laws* on a public subscription channel, or tap into a chat show asking the burning question; *do blondes have more fun?* Or, a programme on obesity declaring, *its fun to be fat!* Or, Home Improvement, Roseanne and Seinfeld every weeknight ... if you can handle the incessant commercial breaks.

It strikes me as it has struck many people before, that this really is a land of striking dichotomies. As I write these words, I have answered the telephone to a psychic offering me astrological and tarot readings on a free 1-800 number, for a small monthly subscription.

You can *buy* God in this country and many people try to do just that! There appears to be a different type of church on all corners of every block and an equally varied people around to attend them.

Yet I love it!

As I stood in a room at Cape Canaveral and marvelled at the old analogue equipment that landed man on the moon in 1969, I realised that few great achievements are orderly affairs with realistic time schedules. I get the feeling that many people look back on great events that they have been involved with and ask ... How? Why? Did it really happen?

I think the answer, is to be prepared for the best at all times. Expect success and it seems that you will be successful. Enjoy now and the future will develop as expected.

Whilst the Americans apparently display extremes of materialism and spirituality, Europeans adopt the stance of an older person looking on at younger people striving to succeed.

We can all learn from one another ... if it were any other way then Darwin's *Theory Of Evolution* would stand up to closer scrutiny. As it is, if survival was the only name of the game then we would all be dead from *terminal boredom* ... because we *can* survive.

We need to evolve and this involves learning ... from within and without!

LIFE IN THE DAY OF

Stimulated by the weekly Sunday Times Colour Supplement articles entitled A LIFE IN THE DAY OF, and written initially for that purpose, but subsequently edited with additions.

Phil Murray is a 43 year old best-selling author of personal development books and audio cassette tape programmes. He lives in Surrey with his wife Allison, 13 year old son Luke and 11 year old daughter Eve. Phil and Allison own a publishing company, a digital recording studio and run the non profit making Positive Attitude Club. They both feel that it is possible to live without believing in anything!

Sleep is a unique opportunity for communion between the various components required in the make up of a human being. I therefore relish alcohol free days which conclude around 21.30 hours, and mornings which begin with the opening of my eyes once again around 07.30.

My thirteen year old son Luke, and eleven year old daughter Eve, invariably join Allison and I in our king size bed for breakfast hors d'oeuvres of freshly squeezed juice and a piece of fruit. We then continue this meal after the fruit has digested, with different comestibles, as we are all in various stages of vegetarianism; from Eve who is totally vegan, to the rest of us who believe in her example, but have yet to make a complete move from diary products. Soya milk is evident, and a weather eye is held on any intrusion into our lives by processed foods filled with preservatives.

Our Border Collie dog Sally, is invited to relieve herself in the humanly unvisited grassy ditches outside the grounds of our house, and seems to relish this exercise as a sensuous experience involving much sniffing and a variety of expressions complimentary to whatever she has sniffed. Now that her nine puppies have all found suitable homes, a modicum of normality has once more enhanced our existence.

After the children have departed for school, I walk Sally and try not to think; rather, I feel that time is useful for staying acquainted with nature. On my return, the computer is switched on, and provided it has booted successfully, I sit facing it with a cup of ginseng tea, ready to record the inspiration which will already be apparent to me, bursting to get out into some form ready for ocular human visitation. The type of material with which I am involved, prevents me from engaging it for too long, and I often find that three hours have passed productively and conclusively.

I then begin my contribution to the business of PeRFECT WORDS and MUSIC. I receive many letters, and constantly distinguish them between those addressed to me as a commercial writer, and those intended for my attention as Leader Of The PAC(K); PAC being an acronym for Positive Attitude Club. I could not resist affording myself this title as head of the non profit making organisation which sprang from my personal development books and tapes, which is dedicated to interactive and creative discussion; it is subsidised by myself and the company which publishes and records my books and tapes ... *it is almost a free after sales service for people inspired by my work!*

I regularly contribute to the Internet in a variety of ways; sometimes in the self help forums and often as part of the world community section. I rarely engage in long and complex discussions, preferring to stimulate talks with any such potential, to a speedy and original conclusion. I feel that the World Wide Web has yet to even approximate its true inherent possibilities; perhaps the conclusive ideas for it have not yet been contemplated. Musing of this nature however, does not form part of my purpose and I await the direction of others in these matters.

I meditate daily, and rejoice in my discovery of the wonderful nothingness which is there for us all to experience if we just close our eyes without trying to do or be anything. If there is any message which runs throughout all of my work it is just that experience ... BE.

The children return, Allison and I wind up our activities which exclude them, before dining as a family at 17.00 hours. I was inculcated with the humourous aphorism when first I moved south from the safety of my northern upbringing, that, *only dogs and northerners have dinner at lunch time.* Tempting though it is to retain a midday dinner time as an attempt at individuality, I have lived down south longer than I lived up north and do not. Perhaps early evening meals are however, a habit left over from our Geordie Tea Times; Allison and I were born and met in Tynemouth, but more likely is the fact that we enjoy sleeping after all food has digested successfully. This allows our sleep time energies to devote themselves in areas other than the stomach. We often read books whose subjects are invariably linked to

Theosophy, Esotericism, The Occult, or titles containing some kind of mystical nuance relevant to whatever personal development process we are undergoing at a particular time.

Evenings are spent either focalising a PAC(K), attending a study group guided by our Flemish storytelling friend Nico Thelman, or watching a movie via a satellite channel. Educational programmes which we enjoy are infrequently broadcast, and we therefore rely on inspirational encounters with our friends for stimulation of this category. A conversation between Nico, another artist friend of ours called Ginger Gilmour, Allison and myself, would customarily contain conflicting data; we always celebrate that difference and aspire to learn from each other. If this is called a social life then we have one. I know it as different to the norm however.

The garden is another joy we are fortunate enough to work and contemplate. We learn much from the simplest and least complicated aspects of nature, but it is application of knowledge to effect change for the better in each of our lives, that I constantly urge all those friends I encounter through the PAC to engage. I affirm this requirement regularly, as I noticed many people enjoyably reading my books and listening to my tapes, without applying the concepts contained in this work to enhance their survival.

Allison and I often laugh at the paradoxes and contradictions contained in the world of personal development, for without them we would all have cognited on the answer to everything, resulting in an eked out existence filled with boredom and purposelessness ... *perhaps!* I do not believe in beliefs, and urge whoever is within my sphere of influence to rid themselves of this mental dead weight whenever an opportunity arises. As I have no opinion about anything, at least as an aspiration, writing becomes a greater challenge. If I espoused extremist viewpoints I would achieve far more publicity than I do, so I don't, because I could! My work is considered to be of minority interest, yet I sell more products in the United Kingdom than any of the more well known personalities frequently imported from the United States. Sales are of minor interest to me and enter the equation only because the *message platform* is frequently and unfortunately more important than the *message,* for without it, who would hear the message!

To conclude with a relevant *don't believe in beliefs* contradiction, I believe in love and warm thoughts, and when utilised with a liberal sprinkling of forgiveness, mountains move, miracles occur and humanity progresses. True human potential is there for us all to access, and it is often inspiration which stimulates the seeking of a path into this realm. If my work accomplishes even a lower harmonic of that concept which I describe, then I may be deemed successful.

I always sleep well.

LITTLE BILLY AND THE BIG HEAVY

The title of anything is usually more important than whatever it refers to, from an attention grabbing point of view. Sad though this may seem to those who have yet to come across this shortcoming of human exploration, it is the case wherever I look. In my universe, and the one which I share with my readers, this means that YOU CAN ALWAYS GET WHAT YOU WANT is a superior book to BEFORE THE BEGINNING IS A THOUGHT, EMPOWERMENT and THE 49 STEPS TO A BRIGHT LIFE, because it has a more attention grabbing title? Using this logic I should call this book you are now reading, something like PHIL MURRAY BITES YOUR BUM OFF, because that is a pretty good title too!

When *in store book-buyers* are deciding the worth of a book to order for their shelves, thus making it available or not for you the reader, they usually feel the cover whilst looking at it, ask its generic description ... PERSONAL DEVELOPMENT in this case ... how much it retails for, and then pronounce their decision. We have sold masses of books to the central buying departments of major high street chains, without any content ever being considered, except for the odd salient point, or bold type which can be seen when flicking through a title using the old *make pictures move that are drawn on postcards* fashion. Using this purchasing method, we could triple the sales of Bibles by re-titling the book DEATH AT EASTER, chivvy along slow titles like James Allen's AS A MAN THINKETH, by calling it SHUT YOUR FACE AND OPEN YOUR MIND, and perhaps make a best-seller out of Voltaire's CANDIDE, by cleverly naming it A FRENCHMAN'S POLITICAL GUIDE TO SEX, MONEY AND TRAVEL.

Thankfully, in the case of PeRFECT WORDS and MUSIC products, your safeguard against rubbish is built into our modus operandi, but this superficial judgement system inevitably means trouble in every aspect of life it touches. For the publishing company which falls under my sphere of influence, this also means judging the fine line constantly, at one side of which lies truth, and the other which holds more rapid money, less satisfaction, more quick sales, less long term growth and ultimate destruction.

The equation is further complicated by the fact that packaging *is* often a representation of what is less visible. For instance, the way you appear *is* a reflection of what you *really* are inside. What most of us tend to do therefore is *treat the symptom*. If your appearance is a little trying on the eye, it seems that a trip to the hairdresser, barber, beauty salon or plastic surgeon is the obvious thing to do which will remedy your imperfections. Yet any one student of the mind knows that ...

> What you are is what you have been
> Contemplating privately
> Secret thoughts come straight to view
> As your surroundings mirror you
> The world is merely what goes on
> Inside your own cerebrum
> *Phil Murray*   (first published in BEFORE THE BEGINNING IS A THOUGHT)

If we know this to be so, then why bother with the superficial make over? It is important to be presentable in this society, but not to substitute personality improvement for character development. The latter is a soul quality which can be utilised after this lifetime is through ... some would even say that character improvement along with experience is the only reason for physical incarnation ... the former personality type life being a flippant and transient illusion.

Witness the person of character, who on close scrutiny has no media type beautiful face, yet exudes charisma and is a joy to be around. The woman who refuses to conform with modern ideas on her sex and appearance, yet appeals to all nearby as a friend. I could list many examples, and you will have images of your own which will satisfy and prove this point too.

Yet again, in harmony with the book EMPOWERMENT, balance is the order of each day. The cover must be good, but this is only relevant if the contents are even better. The title should represent within, but if it is duplicitous and conniving, the truth will eventually show itself. I call on all to cease eye fluttering at the flimsy world of physical make believe, and prompt a move on invisible truth. *All fur coat and no knickers,* summed it up for generations of us northerners on a purely physical level; *all show and no substance* was another way of putting it; *don't judge a book by its cover;* but I think the time has come to introduce a little computer-speke ... let us all aspire to being true physical representations of ourselves by concentrating within and awaiting reflection without ... **WYSIWYG** ... *what you see is what you get.* Put it on you business card and never again pretend to be something you are not. It is amazing just how much stress will fade from your universe the minute you implement this dynamic little lesson.

Now, what was I saying about Little Billy And The Big Heavy?

LONDON

So, I was asked to focalise a Positive Attitude Club in London and accepted the invitation with pleasure. I did not know the lady who offered to organise the event, and certainly had no idea who would be interested enough to attend from her sphere of influence; I therefore mailed out to all London PAC members and offered them the opportunity to partake of an evening which had all the potential of whatever they were willing to give!

A regular 1½ hour journey from my area of Surrey to North London lasted 2¾ hours; caught in the peak time traffic and crawling over Hammersmith Bridge at painful pace, Allison called ahead to inform the host of our possible lateness, which eventually turned out to be only a few minutes. The 1996 European Football Championship Semi Final between England and Germany was to be played during the same time period the PAC would happen. No one had thought of that when the date was set two months prior. Jingoism was rampant in television magazine type programmes, along with all the usual garbage tabloid newspaper headlines, and I looked forward to my privilege of presenting an idea for interactive potential, whilst the English and Germans slogged it out on the pitch ... *forward thinking through creative discussion,* was the message I sent through to the organiser when asked what they should expect of a PAC.

I arrived with a smile and announced that a very important rule in personal development which I recorded in my third book, is to not ever be late for an appointment once made ... *this evening,* I continued humourously, *may I also remind you all that there is no such thing as absolute anything, and this is why I am late.* There were three men present and many more ladies; *the football,* I thought, as I perused a circle of potential new friends. I realised quite quickly, and the thought was telepathically acknowledge by Allison, that this group were not used to being addressed by the type of manner which is inherently mine.

I urged everyone to ponder the words and ignore the carrier of them, for if we are to make progress, stimulation, inspiration and information are all available from a variety of sources which we may not like in themselves. It soon became apparent as more information about this group, who mainly knew each other, was forthcoming, that they were used to attending weekly new age type lectures. I am conversant with the type of event to which they had grown accustomed, and they are a far cry from what I was suggesting, half presenting and trying to focalise with them that evening.

During this type of lecture with which they felt comfortable ... the Shaman demonstrates, the Historian lectures his linear thoughts about the formation and destruction of Atlantis, the Chiropractor criticises the doctor whilst extolling the virtues of spinal study the modern way; the Neuro Linguistic Programmers talk about change, with methods formulated and stimulated from studies of Milton Erickson, a hypnotherapist, Fritz Perls, the originator of Gestalt Therapy and Virginia Satir, a fairly well known family therapist; the secrets of Hawaii and the Huna, using money as a friend, the truth shall set you free, heal the world, the ancient Vedas, the Native American Indian, Relationships, The Celestine Prophecy, Colour Therapy, Right Living, Inner Peace, Life Dynamics and of course many variations on Awakening the Giant, Power, Truth and Real You within.

They were used to backslapping and affirmations of the way they were, with a patronising backward glance on the rest of society who have not yet seen the light. They had become as comfortable in their new age world of light, as *the others* were with their old age world of apparently not so light. This reminded me of the good old long haired 1960's hippie who delivered tirades about capitalism and the establishment during youth, yet now works in a High Street bank suffering baldness. *What you resist you become,* is an old saying I recall, and these people had found a new age comfort zone which was affirmed each time they met and gloated on *their* knowing, and others *not* knowing.

I asked them what real and long term impact their association with new ideas, new age, new ways and new this, that and the other, had on their lives, and the not quite verbalised answer which emerged was *none*. They had merely substituted old beliefs for new, much as had happened in the story of Aladdin with the lamp. I suggested that we could all live without beliefs and opinions, but most of them associated their beliefs and opinions with their very identity. By this time my words were now almost threatening, as I challenged them to rid their universes of all opinion and belief that was no longer serving them well, and at this time the room became uncomfortable.

A lady in the corner mentioned her anger at a television programme which had presented an unbalanced viewpoint of Homeopathy. *How will your anger effect positive change in your life and the world,* I asked, before she fell asleep. A former Marxist objected to my use of the word *we*, when discussing forgiveness of a violent rapist, and asked who I was including when using it ... *whoever wishes to be included, but definitely not you,* was my reply. A lady to my left, asked me to cease referring to former PACs, as she felt these references made this PAC less valid ... *oh boy* ... I pushed button after button ...

That evening was not designed to be a comfortable night out instead of the television; effecting worthwhile change is not necessarily fun, ridding yourself of beliefs is not easy, ceasing opinions can be a painful experience. If these changes were easy, would not more people be trying them as a quick fix, like turning on a light switch? Oh, and then there was the chap who came along for the ride with a PAC member, who asked for a cup of tea, when a general question from Allison was presented to the group as to what everyone expected from the evening. He smelled of alcohol and left for a cigarette after fifteen minutes, not to return until the event had passed. *He's writing a personal development book,* his friend announced gleefully.

My words are not designed for spoon fed groups or individuals who have been slapped on the back so many times they are afraid to step out of a comfort zone no different to the one they criticise other *less cognisant* individuals for having.

London, Paris, New York, Munich, it doesn't matter where you are from, a cosmopolitan viewpoint is no guarantee that personal development will be any easier for you than it will be for the country yokel who contemplates during milking time. Do not confuse your social condition with that atmosphere which lurks in your inner world. Change means change! If you are not ready for it don't flirt with it. Should your decision be to stay comfortable, set in your own beliefs, surrounded by your long standing affirmations and to continue celebrating your difference with the rest of the world, then stand clear of the doors as they close out the effective potential only accessed when true change for the better, is invoked by *actually* changing.

MORDY VISITS THE ISLANDS

He didn't like holidays much at all. He didn't take kindly to change. The problem was connected to business momentum and his middle eastern upbringing. He was programmed for profit and there was none to be had from these nonsensical breaks on which his wife insisted from time to time. *You want the seaside*, he once said whilst showing her a picture of Tel Aviv beach, *look at this while smelling some fish!*

They now had a child, the production of which had been necessary to retain his English wife in matrimony; she provided him with cheap service and passive complicity. Her nationality had also guaranteed his immigration status, which up until their marriage had been the object of profuse lies and time wasting manipulations of the over stretched resources of the United Kingdom's immigration service. The excuses for presenting his spouse with no more children, along with the lies which produced the immigration visa, were as creative as his life ever became. Mordy left a trail of destruction behind him, which was never quite tangible enough for anyone to accuse him of much, other than causing sadness, misery and nasty thoughts with whomsoever he came into contact.

He found a way of buying lots of property without ever really owning it. He charged exorbitant rents, and celebrated whenever a government agency funded the living expenses of his under privileged tenants. He was universally hated by all who knew him, excepting for those who aspired towards such behaviour as was his, in their own lives; these people quietly tolerated him in an effort to extract his modus operandi for their own future and selfish little ends, but would have sold his life for a couple of beers.

It was curious that he was unable to spend any profits from his tiresome schemes comfortably, but this of course was the universal justice often called karma quietly doing its self levelling job for nature. The child learned all that his father knew by mere association; this enabled the line to continue with its traditions for yet another generation, although it would have pleased the father more had the son been gaumless and incapable of such comprehension. More power to the father through ignorance of others, was the thought which hazily yet persistently passed through Mordy's unevolved and sick little mind, whenever he contemplated the free lessons his son gained through living with him.

Mordy, his wife and son, had driven to Penzance from the

Home Counties, in their extremely old estate car. This saved them money and cost them tiredness. Weariness was free, as was the shocking behaviour of the son in his bid for rest. There were various schemes for crossing the Atlantic to the Isles of Scilly, none of which suited Mordy. The threat of divorce once again forced his hand; two adults and one child subsequently found their way onto the ship for a short crossing.

Mordy was more miserable than usual, and the bright sunshine did little to alleviate the stress which was now quite apparent in his every expression. He found a dark, cool corner beneath decks and smoked his pipe. The no smoking sign was mentioned by more than one passenger, but Mordy merely grunted a fearful sound to each of them and their comments; no trouble was sought by fellow passengers who were mainly happy to be on holiday, and Mordy sank deeper into a depression.

Unbeknownst to him, his wife purchased tickets for entry into the sub tropical gardens at Tresco, one of the larger islands in the group. These tickets also covered them for the short inter island transfer by motor launch which would be necessary to take advantage of that purchase. He slyly nipped her in anger, whilst smiling for the benefit of those observing his uncouth behaviour. He spent the remainder of that voyage, which others found stimulating and enjoyable, obtaining a refund for the child's ticket. *We can get away without paying for him,* he barked at his wife before pocketing the rescued £1.50.

The ship docked in Hugh Town harbour on St Mary's, and passengers for Tresco transferred onto the small launch which would take them across to their destination. There was a distinct and antiquated carnival type atmosphere which greeted their arrival; the ship carried the Royal Mail and was treated with great respect by the islanders. Mordy grimaced at their naiveté and simplicity, but something was slowly fighting its way into the wasted consciousness which was his for life.

He observed the friendliness and what he called lack of drive, in all who had greeted their arrival. The young man asked for their tickets on the inter island transfer launch, and when he began his customary misleading explanation as to why one was not needed for his son, the collector merely smiled and said, *we don't worry about things like that here sir!* Mordy accepted the free ride for his son and smiled back to the ticket collector, but the smiles were not related in any way shape or form, except for the fact that they caused both facial expressions to change for two different reasons.

Mordy would profit from this day trip! He arranged to meet up with his wife and child back at the Mermaid public house on St Mary's, to where he returned immediately. He ordered a small orange juice, lit up his pipe, and he was soon in conversation with local tongues far looser than was his. He never drank alcohol, always stayed sharp and rarely enjoyed himself. The locals noticed his wallet bulging with cash as he paid for the drink, and he proudly boasted to them that he always carried at least £1,000 in cash with him wherever he went; that way he was always available for a deal.

There was an old widow to the south side of Hugh Town called Mrs Hicks, he heard jovially in that conversation, who thought she needed to sell her house quickly so that she could be with her daughter in Cornwall, whose husband had abandoned her three months before their baby was due. The locals were all laughing at the story, but Mordy had heard enough.

Within two hours a deal had been struck between that woman and Mordy which favoured the latter so heavily, that even he could not contain his delight. He was able to describe her property as being so much in need of repair, an impossible sale to any except himself, and in such a poor location, that she was positively giving thanks to her guardian angel in front of him, for sending a saviour her way. Mordy was used to this reaction however, and played to it like a real showman, always making his victim feel good about what had passed and what would be. Mrs Hicks signed a letter of intent in Mordy's favour, and Mordy did the same for her.

He spent the remainder of his wait for wife and child, bargaining through chance meeting, with a fellow day-tripper, for a ring he had noticed earlier on that man's hand during the crossing. Three futile hours were wasted on that piece of jewellery, whose owner did not have the foresight to tell Mordy immediately that it was not for sale. Once back at the Mermaid, he was soon in conversation once again with the same local tongues who fortuitously only a few hours previously had apparently saved the day for him. More alcohol had slurred their speech a little, but the atmosphere had noticeably changed for the worse ...

"You bought that house we told you about then," asked an old fisherman who only hours earlier had laughed and joked with Mordy about him being cosmopolitan and them being simple island fisher folk.

"Of course," replied Mordy, "it is against my nature to let such a deal go to waste."

"But the deal would not have gone to waste my friend, it would only have taken a little longer for the right buyer to come along," continued the fisherman.

"I am the right buyer," insisted Mordy.

"Not for the islands you are not my handsome," interrupted a boatman friend of the fisherman's, "there's nothing in this deal for anyone except you! Old Mrs Hicks showed that letter of intent you signed for her to my friend here, who has given it to me for close scrutiny."

"It's a free country isn't it," was Mordy's clichéd reply, as he showed a little concern at their speedy knowledge of what he thought had been a confidential negotiation, "how did you know about it so soon anyway?"

"News travels fast in these small communities," answered a third member of the local drinking party, "that's part of the islands beauty, and one big reason why they stay so beautiful. You dropped her price too much and we are asking you to reconsider!"

"No we are not," interrupted the fisherman, "we're bloody well telling you to take your city money and stick it where it does no harm ... "

"Where the monkeys stick their nuts," shouted a voice from behind the bar, "and were the sun doesn't shine," added another, not satisfied with the use of only one well worn phrase to describe their feelings for Mordy's fiscal manipulations.

The ship's hooter was sounding for the last time before it would return to Penzance, and Mordy, showing uncharacteristic concern for the continued absence of his family, asked if they had been seen.

"He's seen them," volunteered the fisherman whilst pointing to the boatman.

"That's right I have and he ain't lying," admitted the boatman after taking a long drink of warm beer, "I say he ain't lying!"

Mordy looked at them all and realised he had to act quickly and with little or no help from the locals. Running out of the pub, randomly asking all he passed if they had spotted his wife and child, it quickly dawned on him that he must call the police, but when he enquired in the bread shop as to their whereabouts, he was informed that there were only two policeman for the islands and they had gone fishing, *if* the ferry had left. Mordy rushed over to the quayside only to see the ship slowly moving away from her berth.

He went back to the Mermaid and shouted out in anger to the local drinkers ... "are any of you going to tell me where my wife and child are?"

"I was just about to as you ran out of the pub," answered the boatman. "When I found out about you and old Mrs Hicks," he continued, "you and that house of hers that is, it was just before I had to do my last run to Tresco. We and the lads here had a quick chat and decided that much as we dislike causing trouble, we'd have to in this case, so I left them there on the jetty, knowing full well you'd all miss the ferry."

"I'm not stupid," began Mordy, reconciled to his downward mobility in the influence stakes amongst his present company, "I won't buy the house, I promise, I won't buy it! You win okay. Here is the letter of intent that she signed for me. Look, I'm tearing it up. Mrs Hicks doesn't want it this way though and she'll hate you all for what you are doing ..."

"Old Mrs Hicks don't know what she wants at the moment Mordy," said the fisherman, "but she don't want you that's for certain. Now, here's the deal ... the bar man there has three tickets for the last helicopter this evening to the mainland. Give the man £200 including his commission and they are yours. Then you pay the boatman another £100 for the special trip he'll have to make over to Tresco to pick the young un and your misses up, and finally, so old Mrs Hicks don't get too upset about all this, you can give me another £200 to cover her expenses for a trip to see the daughter, so she can explain that she isn't selling up no more; to no stranger anyways."

Mordy did all that was asked of him, knowing that to refuse would be futile. Once reunited with his family, and far worse off than when they had all arrived that morning, the boatman escorted them safely to the helicopter, which they boarded just as it was ready to take off. Before the door closed, Mordy shouted to the boatman ... "how come you are so sure you did the right thing then. You didn't think I was the right buyer ... you didn't think I was paying enough for the house ... you said that old Mrs Hicks doesn't know what she wants at the minute ... you tell me she isn't selling now anyway ... are you lot the judge and jury all together in one drunken group then?"

"Don't worry yourself now Mordy," shouted the boatman with a smile, "old Mrs Hicks is my mother in law. I only came here for the season and I'll be back with her daughter in Cornwall by autumn. I was born here on St Mary's see ... these islands get into your blood; when me and the misses had a rough time on the mainland I run for home. I've had time to think and I'm going back to put things straight and bring her and the new baby back here where we belong. Old Mrs Hicks will know soon enough. We want to buy her house for ourselves you see, and she can live with us. We decided just before I ran away for a bit. We're the right buyers Mordy; keep island property for the islanders is what we always say!"

The stewardess asked Mordy to take his seat as the noise rose to a crescendo. "Keep your hand on your holiday money and don't sign nothing," shouted the boatman facetiously to Mordy, as the door swung shut and the helicopter lifted into a clear blue sky. "Don't sign nothing," repeated the boatman as he climbed back into the launch, counting his money and re-reading the letter of intent Mordy had signed for Mrs Hicks. *That's a lot less than what we was going to pay for it,* he thought to himself.

MR MIRE
a story containing potentially offensive allusion

THE JUDGE

So, ladies and gentleman of the jury, you have heard the evidence, and it is now your duty to hear a summary from both the defence and the prosecution, before retiring for contemplation of it as a group. I expect a quick judgement; this case should not ever have reached such a high court, and I heartily believe that in this day and age of peace and understanding, time wasting as this matter undoubtedly is, will quickly become a thing of the past. As you are presenting your own defence Mr Mire, do speak first and be brief!

MR MIRE ... reading from a note

Well your honour, may I respectfully request that we hear a summation of these serious allegations from the prosecution first. That way I will be able to more accurately target my response.

THE JUDGE
Very well.

THE PROSECUTION

Your honour, Mr Mire has not denied that on the 1st January 2000, one of the very first altercations with which he was involved, was an undoubtedly premeditated and offensive outburst in a public place, of language which deeply shocked the mixed gathering of party revellers, as they all welcomed, in their own way, the new millennium.

The defence quite honestly is laughable. To say that the addition of extra consonants denotes an entirely different meaning to basic swear words, curses and insults, is a semantic stretch of anyone's imagination.

I call for a period of imprisonment, and feel sure that your honour will consider the maximum sentence, should this fine jury find, as we all know it will, Mr Mire guilty.

I leave the matter with you all and rest my case.

THE JUDGE
　Mr Mire ...

MR MIRE
I might not be educated like the honourable man who has just spoke your honour, and from now I'll not use me notes as has been me habit. I've looked up the word semantics in the court dictionary, and a think that word just aboot sums up me own words. Mr Mire picks up the dictionary and reads from it. Semantics ... *concerned with the meanings of words.*

That's me point your honour and people of the jury. I stood on the toon hall steps at haf past midnight and shooted at the top of me voice, *fluck of you flucking clunt.* I'm fifty five years old, I'd had a lousy life until a discovered in 1999, that a could dee sumit aboot it; sorry ... *do something about it.* I made a millennium resolution to never swear again in me life, so when a got emotional aboot the new year, and looked back at fifty five stinking rotten years of nowt, a had to shoot sumit, so a was shootin at meeself man, a *wasn't* shooting at the coppa like he said a was.

Now you lot have to decide if me adding *l* into these words, takes away the offensiveness. Am ganna tell yi this ... *l* or no *l*, it is the intention behind the words a used, that is what yi should be lukin at man. A just wanted to shoot. That's wot a was brought up to dee yi na. If *fluck of you flucking clunt,* is still offensive to yis, then giv is a bit more time ti lorn and al see worra can dee.

　Alrite?

THE JUDGE
Thank you Mr Mire, I think we understand your meaning, however colloquial its transmission may have been. You are asking us to consider the intention behind your words as a senior point in question to that of the actual words used by you on this occasion.

Ladies and gentlemen of the jury, we await your decision.

The Story Of This Work ... *so far*

The process recommenced way back in April 1976, when I was introduced to some new ideas, and a technology that was way ahead of what I had been able to contemplate on my own up until that time. Before that, my interest in human potential had surfaced briefly as a teenager, when a friend and I would retire to our rooms in adjacent bed-sits, and unsuccessfully perhaps, practice telepathy. The organisation responsible for the furtherance of this technology to which I was introduced in 1976 however, soon showed itself to be unstable, as did some of the ideas.

The seed had been planted and watered within me however; I believe the years that intervened between 1984 and 1993, held purpose which always hovered around the subject of learning *how to know*. What happened on the 2nd of January 1993, is well documented in the book, YOU CAN ALWAYS GET WHAT YOU WANT ... in a nutshell ... the watered seed was warmed by *the sun* of an old friend and the blossoming process began.

Personal Development

I studied the subject thoroughly and found the complete gamut of ideas that I held within myself, loosely disseminated by, and scattered between, around twenty authors and teachers, most of whom were American. At an American Independence Day party given by the old friend who had warmed the seed, I casually mentioned to his colleague that I intended to record a self help programme of my own. I planned to utilise my production knowledge in the audio field, to produce an audio cassette tape programme of superior quality from both a technical viewpoint, and as I felt later, a content viewpoint, to those that were available at that time.

The cassette programme recorded well, and I began to rewrite and lengthen the audio script into a manuscript. This allowed me to add more data, including information of a nature that would have been less easily assimilated had I included it in the original audio format. Both the book and tape are called YOU CAN ALWAYS GET WHAT YOU WANT.

The PAC, came into being firstly as a concept to help impart the ideas in my work, and then as a physical manifestation which now meets at least monthly in the modern workshop fashion. More groups are being contemplated as an expansion to the physical concept ... and I believe the mental aspect of the PAC is proving itself to be a simple solution to everyday challenges occurring in the lives of many PAC People.

I wrote about *The Ether Waves* and *Premier Imagination,* only to discover that the more I contemplated them from a writing and reporting perspective, the more I was in touch with these qualities from a personal point of view. The personal gain occurred in quantum leaps.

The Marketplace

On discovering that most personal development I came into contact with was geared toward business advantage, I noticed people embracing the subject and departing from it without any personal gain whatsoever. This helped me arrive at the realisation that this loose generic title of PERSONAL DEVELOPMENT had indeed become abused.

The Chinese Meal Syndrome, of being *satisfied for but a short time only,* which I mentioned light heartedly in the first book, was taking on a more serious connotation. I felt that as most people were demanding *The Quick Fix,* many Personal Development Teachers were giving way to these demands in direct contrast to their own convictions.

Eventually I discovered a writer and philosopher who espoused in books and tapes, some of the feelings that I held within. I studied him and was eventually asked to work with the dissemination of his material. Unfortunately, I discovered in the nick of time yet another challenge ... *Interpretation.*

The people whom I had planned to work with had assimilated the philosophy only as it had agreed with their own personality's upward mobility. The subject of *Interdependence,* meant little more than the old way of people working for one another. *Trust and Trustworthiness* translated to a deep suspicion of intentions, and *Philanthropy and Altruism* were seen as softness leading to failure.

The Escape

I have a friend working in the dissemination of this philosophy who constantly advised me to remain independent of it; I kindly translated that advice within the spirit of that philosophy to *remaining interdependent from a distance* ... for the time being.

The ideas for the second book, BEFORE THE BEGINNING IS A THOUGHT, began to take a pleasing form ... I had decided to create a bridge between enthusiasm for personal gain, (YOU CAN ALWAYS GET WHAT YOU WANT ... *the body*) and the route to real success. The only way I could do this was through concentrating on the simple PAC Philosophy and working with it hand in hand. BEFORE THE BEGINNING IS A THOUGHT became the middle part of my *body, mind spirit trilogy*. The final work is called EMPOWERMENT, the spirit book which I felt at the time would conclude my involvement in creating a success programme for modern day life.

It didn't!

The Continuance

Something was still lacking ... I wrote THE 49 STEPS TO A BRIGHT LIFE, which addresses the fundamental reason for being incarnate on this planet. *To tell our own unique stories through living* ... is my simple description in that book of true happiness. This book BITES then had to be written as it would not leave me alone. I set aside 1996 as a year of business development, but by the month of March I was writing daily, and in line with my own personal story, I was *happier for it!* My contemplations were finally released from its clutches just before 1997 descended, and now realise that just as I have described a person's involvement with personal development being eternal, so too it almost seems for me is writing about it.

As I write, we now have five books, an assortment of related audio cassette tape programmes and the Positive Attitude Club, scheduled to run until the year 2193. The club and all of its associated material point in the direction of much more worthy and deeper work which exists for all who seek it. Where we go from here depends on you!

NLP AND ALL THAT

In the early 1970's, the formulation of earlier studies by its founders, became known more widely as Neuro Linguistic Programming, subsequently shortened to NLP. I include a bite of information and observation about this subject, because it regularly crosses my path in various guises.

John Grinder, then an Associate Professor of Linguistics at the University of California, colluded with Richard Bandler, a mathematician, Gestalt therapist and computing student, to hatch forth the sum of their mutual studies observing three successful therapists, using videotape, and, whenever possible through closer perception in person. The three people they studied were Fritz Perls who originated Gestalt therapy, a successful family therapist called Virginia Satir, and their best known mentor Milton Erickson, who was a hypnotherapist.

Their initial object was to identify and isolate successful patterns utilised by prominent therapists, in order to cut through long study time students normally endured, by transferring already tried and tested techniques straight on to them. Building models of ready made success that others could copy was an idea that forms the basic building block of all NLP techniques. A greater enjoyment of life was anticipated for users of NLP, along with more effective communication, and enhanced ability to change for the better ... and accelerated learning techniques. All approaches seemingly to me, quite inorganic and opposite to my idea of a fulfilling life.

Mirroring, matching, re-framing, pacing and anchoring are all words used to describe various exercises which are taught quite often to new age groups, and whenever possible to fee paying businessmen. The technology has practical uses in counselling and business it seems, and certainly is useful for an overview of education systems. It is a fast growing industry of applied psychology; that being so it relates only vaguely with the personal development aspect of life to which I address.

It is my experience that most people are interested in NLP for their own selfish ends. It is a technology which enables you to control the response another will have to a given communication or action. If they are visually oriented people, you address them as such ... *do you see what I mean ... I see what you are doing.* This raises the affinity and reality level between communicatees, but in a false and lifeless way. There is a total absence of *vive la difference* in this equation, and more a tendency to *mort la difference.* People who communicate their way through life preferring sound would be treated to parrot fashion phrases like, *I hear what you say,* and, *listen to this report.* The area of kinaesthetics covers those of us preferring the sensory track through life using touch and motion ... *do you get a good feeling about this ... let me run this past you.*

Mirroring can get someone who would have no reason to notice you, and perhaps does not even know you, to have immediate affinity for no apparent reason. I have experimented with this technique with a girl on a train and can vouch for its worth ... DANGEROUS IN THE HANDS OF THE UNSCRUPULOUS! Techniques available from a book by Bandler and Grinder called FROGS INTO PRINCES, make it possible for a person to contact areas of their life which could be deemed problematic, even in front of a group, as any problem does not have to be verbalised, and it is feasible to achieve a physical response to this address. This works too; I have experimented with it and achieved such physical response. Whatever was happening however, was not under my mental or spiritual control. It was a physical response, and as such I find the technique wholly unsuitable for true personal development, which requires full knowledge of all that occurs on the personal path of progress. Even the healing of a cut, accelerated by NLP technique, is less valid than the organic healing of that same cut when a better learning process is connected to it.

NLP, which addresses the way a person views life, is effective in as much that it brings about an awareness of potential. A thinking individual would be able to take this new found awareness elsewhere and find it more than just a little useful. The teachings connected with mind maps are helpful, and the metaphor that *the map is not the territory,* is an excellent way of describing to someone that the way they see a part of life is not necessarily how that aspect of life really is.

My worst experience of NLP, was having an old friend who had just completed a course, mirror me all the way through dinner. What he didn't realise was the fact that I was planting actions for him to mirror. If I had picked my nose whilst eating desert, I swear he would have done so too. It all became a stupid and pointless game. Just as is selling a car to someone who does not really need it; you can if you want, but because you can you shouldn't! I need not describe NLP much more, as those readers who have an interest will further it elsewhere

The point is this ... NLP has thrown up some useful metaphors which normal, thinking and evolving human beings can utilise, without ever becoming more fully involved in this very inorganic approach to personal development. In this, it is not dissimilar to many so called new age techniques, tricks, and schemes which have emerged during the twentieth century, and very likely will continue throughout the twenty first century too.

Just about every single sect, cult, religion, club, group or philosophy which has endured fair longevity of operation, must indeed have within it, no matter how hidden and obscured it may seem, an element of truth. My simple esoterically oriented outlook on life, allows me to extract truth from wherever it may live, without feeling a necessity to belong, worship or join, the holder of that wisdom. I think *NLP and all that,* fits into this way of thinking comfortably.

Performance And You At The Half Way Mark

You are half way through this book, or thereabouts, and it is inevitable that you will have noticed some inconsistencies, irrelevancies, paradoxes and conflicts in the material. It is also likely that you have tuned in to the style which I am utilising for this work, and are now able to second-guess what comes next. These possibilities may lead you to believe that the knowledge and *feel* which I seek to impart, is lesser than it is actually, and to experience this, is it seems, human.

The main point to bear in mind is that *I* am totally irrelevant to the nature of these bites of knowledge. As the facilitator of a task only, for you to focus on me as a personality, would be to do yourself an injustice. I write these words through my personality, but here all connection ceases. Without a mind and body, I would be incapable of consciousness on this plane. It is through this unique combination that data is able to be transmitted; this does not mean however, that credit must go to the personality, for it is my soul purpose which is utilising the vehicles mentioned ... now that explanation has removed all possibility of credit being given to me by you, I shall allow myself the exact amount of commendation due, and get on with the job in hand!

The half way mark in this book may also correspond figuratively speaking, with the human age of 49, a period of life when most of us begin to have the potential for more time to ourselves, as families grow and leave home, work has become more predictable, egos are mainly controlled or controllable, and thought has led us to believe that there is more to life than meets the eye.

49 years of age is too old for us to agree upon it as a starting point for personal development however, as the benefits of human progress need to be experienced at more youthful ages ... for this to transpire it is important that younger people be attracted to this

material in order for its dissemination to occur. Until we can have a double period of personal development per week included in the school curriculum, it is a challenge for us to make self improvement attractive to an adolescent generation just experiencing egos and sex and drink and relationships and sport and personality led fashion.

How can we accomplish this?

In bites ... small pieces of immediately experience-able material. The attractive material to this age group will have instant gratification as its fulcrum, and viewable results at its upper end. The visualisation of various forms of success springs to mind as I write these words. If you can describe to a child that *before the beginning is a thought,* and then take them through the process of conceiving and then accomplishing small tasks, this will be enough for some. They in turn will take it upon themselves the task of relating this miraculous potential to their contemporaries. A few will hold back and keep it to themselves, as do their older generation counterparts, and to those who do this it must be explained that all of this data must flow through us to others, otherwise it solidifies within the mind and body, sometimes even causing illness and disease.

I remember showing my son the art of deciding what you wish to have happen and then making it happen. He was just about to begin a game of football as centre forward. I asked him if he intended to score any goals. He said, *let's just see what happens,* which is ultimately the best way to enjoy a game, but not however, for our purposes at that time. I pursued the point and got him to describe his first goal of the hat trick he had by then decided upon. He told me of a crossed ball from the right wing aimed just perfectly for his head as he stood centre of the six yard box. We were both a little startled when this exact scenario occurred within the first two minutes of the game. He looked over to me with a knowing glance and shouted, *it works!*

Affirmations can transform a fragile little personality into one of growing confidence, until eventually and hopefully, that personality can be transcended. *I am clever ... I look good ... I am creative ... I succeed.* It may feel strange for a youth to embrace these ideas in the first instance, but perseverance is worthwhile if we are to effect a peaceful revolution of human potential sooner rather than later. The danger lies in the fact that we could fill our youth so brim full of confidence and egocentricity, that they fail in transcending the personality to uncover their own true character, or soul purpose. This is the risk we take. If you feel it worthwhile, then teach children the art of forgiveness, affirmations, visualisation, meditation or *TTM, time to myself,* as I have called it throughout my books; focusing, thinking the right thoughts, analogy, metaphors, effective communication, misunderstood words and their power over true understanding, the orientation of humans in order to communicate effectively ... do they prefer audio, visual or kinaesthetic oriented communication; money, personal empowerment, and how it is better to be *interested* rather than *interesting*.

We should aspire towards a youth that will be inspiring for us! Plan your children to embrace personal development data way before you or I would have contemplated it. In doing so you will find a rebounding effect of accelerated serenity and causation creeping into your lives.

Do not concentrate on the personality, look for the soul. Just like looking behind the headlines of a newspaper, if you seek the spiritual qualities of a human being, you will usually find them lurking behind the brazen personality, wondering if it is time to pop out and show itself yet! With encouragement, this should happen sooner rather than later.

At the half way point of this book which you are reading, if you have not cognited on at least ninety five percent of the contents of this bite, it is my humble opinion that you should begin reading the book once again from the beginning, or perhaps grab an earlier piece of my work which may set you up in a more relevant frame of mind for this one.

Personal Development is as easy as you wish ... you have to get down to the business of doing it though. This means getting into action with assimilated data. This means outflowing goodness and blueprinting an ethical life of well meaning plans. This means spreading the word so that the word does not solidify within you causing you to choke before any personal success is forthcoming.

Love *is* the only revolution, but we have to effect many changes before its true potential will shine through ... teaching all you know unselfishly helps *you* more than would at first perhaps be apparent ... I recommend it ... but you have to do it ... not just talk about it!

Just do it!

POLITICS

Sex drugs and rock n'roll brought into being The Monster Raving Loony Political Party during the 1960's, to the delight of myself and many others. British politics were, like most democratic politics world-wide, duplicitous and conniving. As the music revolution unfolded, the contraceptive pill became available alongside so called leisure drugs, and musicians along with all types of artists, were amongst the first to openly take advantage of this new freedom, in what could be described tabloid fashion as drunken debauched orgies of sex, self gratification, and if you were lucky, a degree of self realisation.

Politicians were the first to wrongly realise that an attack on the new age of promiscuity, was a vote winner with the older age groups. Generation clashes abounded, and then the *Profumo Affair* hit the headlines. Yes, the people who afforded themselves the title of moral guardians for our country, were *doing it* too! John Profumo, Member of Parliament, was having an affair with a prostitute called Christine Keiler.

Screaming Lord Sutch was a mildly successful pop singer at the time, and noted the hypocrisy, and also it must be said, clocked an excellent publicity opportunity. He decided to stand against John Profumo at the following election to point out certain flaws in Profumo's utterings, and has been standing as a candidate in elections ever since. He is the longest serving leader of any political party anywhere in the world. Following his stance against Profumo, he then stood against Harold Wilson up in Liverpool, Margaret Thatcher in Finchley many years later, and is still active as I write these words in 1996 ... more than thirty years on.

Now, I have heard him criticised by fellow politicians as taking advantage of the political system, being facetious with democracy, being childish, stupid, impractical and well, well ... light hearted, damn his eyes!

I chanced across BBC Radio Southern Counties the other day and listened to a gentleman called Lord Tiverton talking about politics, and as he had a refreshingly alternative viewpoint I afforded him careful attention. He mentioned four things that Screaming Lord Sutch had listed in his manifestos over the years, only for people to scoff, but which had all borne fruit. He called for *public houses to stay open all day* ... wild at the time but common place now. He said we should *lower the voting age to eighteen;* many politicians laughed, but the voting age is now eighteen. He demanded *an end to the selective eleven plus examination,* which streamed children into different schools. Unthinkable ... well almost ... it was abolished! He said *that radio should not be the preserve of the BBC,* at a time when the organisation was all powerful, and now there has been such an amount of broadcasting deregulation that you can find local radio in just about any town in the country. I am sure he also asked about *shops being open on Sundays* and they now are.

Well, looking back on the words I have just written it strikes me that he is not such a fool after all. In fact the opposite seems to be true, judging by his record, and is that not what we should look at when appraising character.

Talk is easy, but living that talk is what separates the truly cognisant amongst us, from those who pay lip service to whatever topic is fashionable and in the headlines. I am not blindly supporting Screaming Lord Sutch by the way; I use him as an illustration of just how dangerous it is to *not* look behind the headlines. A chap calling himself Buckethead stood in a London election during the 1980's, and I must confess that if I had lived in his district I would probably have voted for him. Why? Because he made people think! Just being there with a bucket over his head was enough to make many of us cast a quick glance over the political arena and remind ourselves that it is still drenched in the stench of hypocrisy and tactics ... and we have one of the best systems in the world!

Long live Buckethead, Lord Tiverton and Screaming Lord Sutch; they have provided a service for us that many politicians can only dream of giving!

Poor Not So Poor And Poorest

Long has it been fashionable to lump all aspects of what we have not, into one neat little labelled bundle. This convenient package is variously marked *poverty, not so well of, deprived, afflicted, under achieved,* and sometimes even *badly done to*. I have experienced interviews of women with small children, standing on the street corners of their *deprived* estates, arguing about which one of them was least well off. That mantle invariably fell to the lady whom had brought most offspring into this world, only to find that the world was not waiting with open arms for these children ... or so popular thought may have it.

Now, when I was a lad living in the heart of shipbuilding Tyneside, poverty was displayed mainly by families who had their attention on things other than any kind of personal enhancement whatsoever. It was usually illustrated by the smell of unwashed clothes and bodies, and the elders of such families were usually to be seen with a fag hanging out of their mouths on the way to a bingo session in the concert hall of the local working men's club; in those days women were rarely allowed in any other room of such establishments.

Amongst the throng of this working class upbringing, the *posh poor* cursed the *less posh poor,* who were recognised as those who paid least attention to new values creeping into those working class circles regarding education. The problem with this new found access to education for even the poorest families, was that as soon as the children had partaken of this right, they immediately wanted to get the hell out of the environment which had afforded them the privilege.

Casting a more distant glance back in time to my Father's childhood, poverty had far graver implications, and death was a frequent visitor to families who had not paid careful attention to health issues. Vaccinations were a thing of the future and two world wars were awaiting their place in history. We can look back further to my Grandmother's time, when it was good to have shoes and be part of a family which did not suffer patriarchal dictatorship inspired by decades of alcohol abuse. We need look no further however, as the word *relative* crosses the meditative path, and we realise that all material poverty is in fact comparative.

It is a fact, that if my family joined up with nine other similarly developed families, and we all took ourselves to live in the most deprived physical environment, we would have an effect not dependent on money or our surroundings for its outcome. If we lived alone as ten new families in a previously run down, filthy, downtrodden rat infested estate, within a matter of weeks, that environment would be transformed to reflect our inner inspirations. If we lived alongside ten other families who had already been living there, hopefully we would at least have a positive effect. If we became the minority alongside twenty other families already living there, we would be tolerated as different. As the ratio decreased, so would our positive effect on that environment. It would fall from total to eventually almost nil.

So it is also in the world of personal development. If you improve yourself, yet remain around enervating people, your progress will be impaired in ratio. Until that is, you cease to concentrate on personality type development, and fix a gaze on true character type personal development; the type you can take with you after this lifetime is over. Once this transformation of viewpoint is ongoing, then life does in fact take on a new meaning ... a deeper significance ... a more wholesome relevance ... a richness.

It will then be found that *the poor* are indeed those of us who have not yet cognited on ourselves as spiritual beings having a human experience. The *not so poor* are that part of humanity living a decent life, yet oblivious to potential beyond their sphere of influence. *The poorest*, are that portion of society who know themselves as powerful spiritual energies, yet do little or nothing for the furtherance of human evolution quickly towards a bright new world.

Such people have sampled their true identity, detected their home environment as the spiritual universe, and even made headway towards eradicating their personality power. The real reason for their development however, has alluded them. Until they turn and look back on those who have yet to begin the great journey which personal development undoubtedly is, and shine a light in that general direction, all future gains will be regularly erased.

Real growth can never be accomplished at the expense of *anything!* It can only be achieved with group knowingness and willing *good for all* within the individual sphere of influence. So, we move the definitions of relative poverty into the spiritual realms, and in these environs we sense that *all* is worthwhile. We sense the great oneness of *all* universal being, and detect that *all* is spirit, from the greatest being whoever *has been, is being and will be,* down to the smallest piece of sand awaiting utilisation into a concrete mix, which itself will form the foundation of a mighty tower block, to eventually become part of an estate people will deface and degrade, whilst they call out for more money, more outside help, more commitment from others, more of everything except their own self determination to rid themselves of the need to seek external help.

Real poverty is all around ... I have witnessed it in Beverley Hills ... I have sampled it whilst staying in the Hollywood Hills ... I sensed it when living in Boca Raton, Florida. It is here in Surrey, England, where I write these words, and most definitely around almost every street corner in London. Real poverty is seen nearby people who do not contribute spiritual inspiration towards general life.

Yet, on Tyneside during the 1950's, as the sirens sounded to herald the end of lunch break for the factory workers, shipbuilders and coal miners, as the seine netters put to sea, amongst the obvious and dismal relative poverty of material deprivation, a *beacon* was so easy to detect. That person who afforded colleagues a smile; the adult who understood and acknowledged the puerile viewpoint as being worthy of hearing; the peer who understood a friends question and was willing to discuss it with them; the teacher who encouraged new determination from a depressing exam failure.

Material wealth does not go hand in hand with spiritual growth. Poverty is not the exclusive domain of the physical universe, and no matter where you find yourself operating, contributions can be made into the universal bank account of goodwill. It is a privilege to make such deposits, and it is a dearth of such action which defines poverty for the 21st millennium.

RELATIONSHIPS

I had a friendly Jehovah's Witness call at my house on more and more frequent occasions. To begin with, the exchanges of ideas seemed quite creative, but it dawned on me that he was quite single minded about the developing relationship.

Single mindedness is often presented as an asset when connected to *always getting what you want* from life, but it must be said that it has its downside. Two way communication cannot occur creatively if a hidden agenda exists. Whenever I asked my friendly Jehovah's Witness a question about any aspect of life, he would show me a passage from the Bible. I have a Bible on my computer and could easily have asked it the same questions and received similar speedy answers as I was hearing from the JW. The conversation I sought was with a person however, and this proved to be difficult in this instance.

Now, I actively work towards a banishment of value judgements about fellow humans, so writing about such things is challenging to say the least; especially when the person you are communicating with is making them on and ever increasing basis, *as the trust grows!*

He told me of his relationship with a local clergyman and his philosophy on points of agreement. This guy seemed obsessed with an interpretation of the Holy Trinity, and made it his business to upset a local Vicar. As this Churchman was closing the door on our friendly JW saying *no thank you,* the JW suggested they find some points of agreement ... *my eyes shone at the thought* ... ten points were described and agreed upon, before the sting was delivered, *which could not be agreed upon* ... about the Holy Trinity.

I suggested that a point of DISAGREEMENT had been sought, before enquiring if wisdom could be gleaned from any other set of beliefs, religions or philosophies? *No,* was the answer; the JW interpretation of the Bible was the only valid one and it was only a matter of time before humanity cognited on this simple supposition.

With stretched patience I suggested that a long period of time elapse before another visit, only to have explained to me that certain maps become available every six months, and although he would not call for a year, someone else may. I felt a certain sadness that my treatment of this JW amounted to little better than most, who slam a door in the face with a verbal obscenity.

Hidden agendas and points of disagreement are the champions of lost causes and broken relationships. Being right is an inferior harmonic to rightness. There are as many different interpretations of the Bible as there are people who have read it ... all are less relevant than any life of *demonstrated* goodness. YOU *CAN* ALWAYS GET WHAT YOU WANT; once you know that and have perhaps demonstrated some simple magic a few times, it will become apparent that there is more to life than *just* getting what *you* want from it.

PEOPLE MATTER MOST, it says in the PAC philosophy, not dogmatism and disregard for other human viewpoints; *an occasional challenge*, you might say!

RESPONSIBILITY

We rapped a good portion of that evening about sound, and the ability to locate oneself apart from the personality. It was stimulating, but we had to maintain the responsibility of allowing all viewpoints an equal amount of credibility. We shared that responsibility superficially, but I had nagging fears about the depth of the true understanding which should have accompanied it. Sure, the lip service was paid, the smiles fell in the right places and positive nods of affirmation were visible, but there was little soul revelation by many individuals in that room.

John, an elderly mystical friend from whom we have all learned happily in a very indirect way, described his feelings experienced during regular, and indeed for him essential, walks into the Ashdown Forest. He identified with each and every sound, and in his special forest place, a location to which I took my Family after his description of it, he felt comfortable and free. He balanced this experience with his dislike of the hustle and bustle of London.

A small contribution from me was to describe my feelings whenever I terminate a train journey to London at Charing Cross Station. Once on the other side of The Strand, I enjoy a feeling of well-being and spiritual connection. As I pass Cecil Court, perhaps on my way to Wardour Street via Leicester Square, the feeling intensifies and I sense that area perhaps as it was during Edwardian Times. Nico added that he was not surprised at my spiritual feelings whilst in that particular environment, as London is one of the five major centres in which an outpouring of spiritual energy is received; the others being Geneva, New York, Tokyo and Darjeeling. He added that his most comfortable surrounding is a city with a pavement underfoot. The environment for most of his life had been the city of Antwerp in Belgium.

John spoke of silence in the country; Ali and I remembered just how noisy we thought it on our first move from a built up area to a more natural space. Dogs barking, birds incredibly vocal as the sun rose, cats screeching in fight, fox noises during the night, lawnmowers, hedge-trimmers, chain saws and of course, the less traffic there is, the more you tend to hear when it appears.

So many assorted ways of perceiving the world and an even greater variety of ways in which we can take responsibility for it. John described a way of locating himself which was stimulating. His bedroom was dark and quiet; each evening after retiring, he would find that silence and darkness an ideal vehicle to aid his perception of him *the being*, as opposed to John the thought bearer incarnate on earth. His description was so simple I found it stimulating. Whether or not he knew it, or intended for it to happen, he was, in that one rendition, taking responsibility for steps along the way, no matter how small, for many of us.

We have a responsibility to recognise each other quite apart from our worldly possessions and images. We have a responsibility to delight in the power we all inherently possess. We have a responsibility to utilise this power carefully, with discretion and a tolerance of other life. We have a responsibility to allow the manifestation of all, with only the slightest of interference when necessary. These descriptions are in addition to the responsibilities we possess which are far more mundane; like paying the mortgage, readying the children for school, cooking the meals, cleaning the house and caring for our families. The difference is that the first descriptions apply to soul qualities and the latter have personality type applications.

Which do we address first?

Any builder will tell you that the most important aspect of any building is the foundations. It therefore follows that by applying the same criteria to individual human life, the aspects you address first will relate to the type of life you wish to lead. If you want a *wham bam zippy fast state of the art fashion conscious jive type existence* then I propose you concentrate on the latter. If you want to follow the spiritual course then you must let your soul be the pilot. One approach does not necessarily lead to the other, but there is no earthly reason why they cannot both exist side by side in a balanced life, and this is the responsibility I describe.

Recognise all that you are and live according to your needs. The ascetic outlook of doing without and sacrificing, is not relevant to any aspect of life with which I am in contact. A positive life of recognition which includes all portions of the human constitution, will allow a far brighter light to penetrate the veil which occludes the mysteries of life of which many of us wonder.

The easiest way to live a balanced life is through a recognition of your identity. You must aspire to become more you, much like others may aspire towards owning a bigger house. Whilst you are becoming more you, you may also buy the bigger house, but it rarely works in reverse. I have yet to discover a person for whom money has bought them a greater spiritual understanding of themselves. Money *can* buy you the time which enables such explorative work to begin or continue, but it is not an end within itself.

Responsibility begins with you, circles your complete sphere of influence before ending with you. There is no escaping responsibility; it is a weak harmonic of that giant universal axiom popularly known as karma. Whether or not you take responsibility for all you should is of course another matter, although it is a fact that the more responsibility you are willing to take, the more responsibility you are able to take.

The choice is and always will be yours!

SALLY

The Murray Family lives with a beautiful Border Collie Bitch called Sally. We tried unsuccessfully, four times to mate her with other Border Collie dogs, but each time the males showed interest, Sally bit them. It seems the time was not right! When she was seven years old, we decided to try one last time, as her age would make any future efforts a little riskier than we felt good about for her first and only litter.

Madison the Border Collie dog, arrived as planned, and they were enjoying each other's company within minutes. It seems the time was right! Nine weeks and three days later, Sally gave birth. During her pregnancy, I read two books about bringing puppies into the world. After ignoring the guilt intended remarks in both books, about how wrong it is for ordinary people like us to allow a bitch to have puppies, when breeders are there to make a living from the process, I felt that I had gleaned enough knowledge to deem myself a parlour expert in the craft of puppy making.

The pregnancy would last nine weeks, I was led to believe ... between 55 and 65 days according to one other book ... whatever, I expected the offspring to arrive nine Fridays after the Friday

Madison successfully accomplished his mating mission. We don't believe in molly coddling our dog, and treat her as we treat each other ... without patronisation. We therefore, have not had occasion to utilise a vet since her initial injections at six weeks old, followed by the last ones she ever had at the age of three months, and we were quite proud of this fact.

Three days later after the date of expectation, I began to feel some kind of *socialisation guilt pressure* at not caring for my dog enough to take her to the vet. I relented, and as she lay on the vets cold linoleum floor, she began to shiver ... the temperature of a bitch drops just before labour begins. I knew this, but allowed the vet to insert a thermometer into her anus anyway; he read the result and pronounced me correct ... but booked her in for a caesarean section the following morning just in case. He was concerned about her size, because our Sally was huge! He also reminded me that more disease preventative injections were vitally important after the pregnancy.

I got her home, took her to one side and suggested it was in her best interests to give birth immediately. She promptly discharged some fluid from her vagina, licked it up, which in turn stimulated another discharge, which itself signalled the onset of contractions ... labour had begun.

The first puppy's ejection seemed to be taking too long. I gently helped it out. As I did so, I really felt like I was meddling in some timeless and majestic process which had been occurring for aeons, and would certainly continue its role, gradually changing with evolution, yet retaining its intrinsic natural rightness, way beyond my foresight of the future. The neighbours dropped in to give support, and we were told when no more were forthcoming after the fifth birth, that she would have this small number because of her age. Once more alone with us, she brought forth another three puppies, making a total of eight. We went to bed after ensuring her comfort, and the next morning there were nine.

I had read that she was to eat no more than two of her afterbirths ... I allowed her to follow instinct and she ate them all ... I shouldn't have done, or so I was told. Water down the milk when weaning them away from the mother ... I didn't. Don't give them solids until they are at least three weeks old ... I gave them solids at two weeks of age. Take them to the vets for a check ... we didn't.

Dos, don'ts, wills, wont's, shoulds, shouldn'ts ... whatever happened to nature. I like a clean environment and swept Sally's whelping area for the first two days after the event ... she may have been smiling to herself at this human response ... Sally ate the solid excrement and licked up the liquid waste that her puppies emitted. In fact Sally did everything for the siblings, constantly cleaning them, licking their genitals to stimulate digestion, and making herself available for feeds at exactly the right time.

You may think we were lucky to have this perfect birth occur for us, but I am sure that it is our constant meddling with natural events that leads to quirks and inconsistencies, disasters and irreverence, in connection with inherent impulses. We have all but removed instinct from the human birthing process. Pregnancy is considered a medical condition by much of society, and not the natural celebration of imminent new life that it undoubtedly is.

I vividly recall the birth of our son. It was our first experience of this process, and like many we decided on natural childbirth. One must clear the definition of *natural,* if you are to possess a successful relationship with those you will come into contact with during, throughout and after the pregnancy. We meant natural ... not just a bit natural ... natural. The pressures were such however, that only the medically proficient amongst us would dare to defy the doctors who insist that grim consequences could be forthcoming should you decide to follow instinct and birth at home.

We arrived at the hospital and Allison was immediately offered gas and air to ease the experience. It was refused, to the dismay of the attending staff. After all went according to plan, and a beautiful son was produced, a new nurse entered the delivery room with a hypodermic needle containing extract of horse's urine, or something similar.

She requested me to move and I asked her why. She explained that she was just about to administer the injection which would allow the afterbirth to be expelled. *Will this not happen naturally,* I enquired, hinting to her that we desired a natural experience. *Not always,* she replied, *and if you do not allow me to administer the injection any forthcoming dire consequences will be your responsibility!* Now, you have to be quite strong after undergoing this birth experience, to maintain your viewpoint when all around suggests otherwise. I managed to sit tight however, and sent the nurse on her way with a smile.

Are we losing touch with our roots? Have we evolved into a race which has disinherited its intuition? How can we live in peace, when war is declared daily on our inner feelings? Should denial of what happens spontaneously all around us herald the dawning of a new spiritual existence without bodies? I don't think so! We find ourselves in that unique position of duality ... spirit and physical body. We have to learn through living, a relationship with the physical vehicle, which satisfies both the body and the soul. The impulse is currently to deny real life in search of some kind of scientific, computer modified, disease free, sterile, impersonal, city based and self seeking existence, where all bows down before the almighty human will and fiat.

If this continues, then I cannot see how we will be able to RESTORE THE PLAN ON EARTH. If we are in constant denial of our globe and all it naturally offers, then at best we can expect to restore the plan on some other planet! There is no such thing as deferred karma however, and we may well wish to shoot off somewhere else where the sun shines bright on the other side, but sooner or later we will have to deal with what is ... and that is ... *life in harmony with all that surrounds us.*

We can monitor the animal kingdom, not with some kind of retrospective evolution in mind; rather, as a spiritual exercise to keep in touch with our physical roots.

Sally taught me that.

SIGH

Someone joined the PAC, sending in a warm and friendly letter full of smiles with their application form. I replied as always, and very soon afterwards a telephone call was forthcoming from this member. The link between myself and this person had been their purchase, reading and enjoyment of the book BEFORE THE BEGINNING IS A THOUGHT; I was asked if it was possible to reproduce part of this book for free in a bi-lingual newspaper, to which I replied in the affirmative. I was further asked if I would agree to write for this newspaper on a fortnightly basis, no fee was discussed or offered, and lastly if I would present a 45 minute talk for the other group to which this person belonged ... without remuneration. I agreed to all requests.

I postponed the Family holiday for a day, and arrived at the venue in which I was to speak. The audience was composed almost entirely of Asians dressed colourfully in national and regional costumes of one kind or another. I was asked to remove my clogs which I did, being used to such requests. My sister is Canadian, outside whose household all shoes must be removed before entering. This practical ritual hails from the time when Canada was mainly dirt with just a few houses, and saved many unnecessary cleaning hours.

The hall filled up and seemed to reach capacity at around 110 people. The females were separated from the males and most sat on the floor. My wife, from where she sat in the female section, emanated a questioning flow my way which I understood. They began to sing in an evangelical manner which promoted a kind of personality type upliftment. I tried to understand the words, and it seemed that they were worshipping some kind of Indian personality who called himself Sai Baba. I had heard of him and his apparent magic, understanding that he claimed to be a reincarnation of the original Sai Baba who had died in 1918. Anyway, it soon became glaringly obvious that these people to whom I would speak were actually devotees of this person who is most well known for seemingly spontaneously manifesting from thin air what many call a sacred ash known as Vibutee, but perhaps not spelled that way, along with watches that a friend of mine explained are actually made in Switzerland.

My wife wondered how I would handle this situation, given that my world was so far removed from the one in which I was to speak. They worshipped, sang and spoke with deep reverence about their hero, as they faced what we in the west would call an altar, covered with religious type pictures and an image of Swami, complete with imagery of his feet at which sat some young girls.

When my turn arrived, I was announced as the personal development author of a book called THE 49 STEPS TO A BRIGHT LIFE, a title which seemed to appeal. The audience clapped and I took up a position in front of their altar, where everyone could easily see, but was asked to stand at the lectern situated on the male side, where a microphone was situated for those who could not hear clearly towards the rear of the hall. I honestly complimented their often beautiful singing, and likened it to the Indian musicals which my wife and I used to watch on Saturday morning television. "We could not understand the words in most songs from those musicals," I said, "but the intended sentiment was transmitted beautifully on a finer flow. What can we learn from this concept in our own attempts at self improvement?"

I invited interactive participation and an exchange of outlooks, but was not asked a single question for the whole of that talk. I spoke of the delicate situation in which I found myself, having to speak about my work, which was quite different from the flavour of that evening, and affirmed that my intention was not to step on anyone's beliefs, which I then inadvertently did without question. I spoke of the potential for living life without beliefs and opinions. I stated my feelings about Gurus ... the fact that if any teacher left a pupil with a feeling of dependence on that teacher, the job of teaching was either not being done properly, or the material within the lesson was sub standard. I spoke about freshly available universal energy in a new age of immense potential relevant to the evolution of humanity. I said that the Christ, Buddhic and any other great energy, is available within each and every one of us, and that no external stimulus was really necessary for personal development and spiritual improvement ... God is everyone ... everyone is God! I shared with them my only one great aspiration which is *to be more myself*. I affirmed what was obvious; that perhaps only twenty people in that audience would benefit immediately in any way shape or form from what I was saying, but that maybe a flavour would remain with the rest, which could be reflected upon during following days.

Believe it or not, my talk under such tense circumstances, overran by five minutes, and the audience clapped nervously when I finished. The old Indian Master of Ceremony's announced rudely, as I was retreating from the altar, that he found my talk "very heavy going," which I felt was a polite way of him verbally sighing, acknowledging that I had not slapped them on the back and affirmed that their way is *the* way, and that everything I had stated during the talk seemed to be the fundamental opposite to their beliefs, and their raison d'être as a group, and calling it crap!

A devotee of Swami followed me as speaker by telling them what they wanted to hear, and very likely what they hear week in week out ... about *his* meeting with Sai Baba, along with stories about Swami and the fact that when asked by a female devotee, who was in awe of him, what type of coffee he drank, as her one question of him, he replied that he did not drink coffee, only a few occasional drops of coconut milk, perhaps affirming for her his self acclaimed status as an Avatar. This provoked shrieks of laughter, as did the fact that Swami occasionally tires of people requesting the manifestation of watches for their possession, when asking his devotees what they want of him, and he regularly must remind them that he offers them spiritual progress when all they want is a new watch.

The PAC member avoided me afterwards, and when I found her to say goodbye she seemed very embarrassed. The organiser muttered something about getting me to do some workshops for the few who may benefit, like he was doing me a favour, and said he would call me. I didn't hear from any of them again, up to the time of this writing that is; no letter of thanks was forthcoming, which is often a traditional acknowledgement for someone who altruistically gives time to groups without financial remuneration and at personal expense, and the first article which I completed for their newspaper did not, to the best of my knowledge, ever appear, and I was certainly not asked to write any more for them.

So a potential audience of many, with a few lashings of my tongue, disappeared from the profit margins of PeRFECT WORDS and MUSIC Limited. Free publicity in their literature was no longer available to me, and some people who may have *adored* me, I felt no longer even liked me. My wife asked quite rightly, in the car as we returned home before commencing our holiday the following morning, if I should not have told them a little more of what they wanted to hear. As she voiced a question that *had* to be asked by one of us, an understanding of my answer coloured her subsequent communications.

"All I have to offer at this moment in time, is exactly what I told them during that speech. To have said anything else would have been a betrayal of myself and the audience. My purpose is not to be liked; rather, to be effective. If an amount of affection is forthcoming of course, it is a bonus, and more than a little welcome," I replied.

When I returned home, I skimmed through BEFORE THE BEGINNING IS A THOUGHT to discover what they had seen in me to begin with, and felt that what I had written in that book was just about the only common ground we had. If they had read the previous book, or any of the following books, they would not have invited me in the first place.

I enjoy what I call forward thinking through creative discussion. To accomplish this one must remove all barriers to communication. Beliefs and opinions *are* such barriers. Group agreements and codes and laws and regulations and dogmas and tenets and doctrines and even thoughts, get in the way of powerfully creative discussion.

Sigh and get rid of them whenever you can!

ps ... just before publication I received a telephone call from the PAC member who organised my speaking at this event; she said that many were moved by what was said, with apologies for not contacting me earlier. A few weeks after that, I was asked to write some relevant words for their new year edition of the mentioned newspaper ... just shows how wrong one can be when jumping to conclusions, second guessing what others may be feeling, and judging a situation ... especially when espousing the philosophy that it is possible to live without doing such things. One can also be very right about such assumptions ... the paradox confronts us once again. I live and learn as do us all ... hopefully!

SILENT KNIGHT PHILOSOPHY AND PERSONAL DEVELOPMENT
an interview with A Silent Knight

Phil Murray
You described your activities in the book Empowerment, as being *the unselfish flowing of Love and Forgiveness into The Ether Waves*. What impact would such outward action have on an individual's inner process of personal development?

A Silent Knight
We, *the Spirit, I AM,* are where and what our attention is placed or focused upon. How can we help but better ourselves if our attention is focused on these two powerful and positive thought-forms of love and forgiveness? Consider the opposite of keeping our attention on negative thought-forms.

Phil Murray
Why do you think such outflow is necessary for humanity?

A Silent Knight
Can anyone doubt that this planet and all life on it is heading in a direction of self destruction? We have been warned for aeons by enlightened ones, regarding consequences of unethical and solely materialistic thoughts and behaviour ... that horrid word *sin* comes to mind ... apparently we think we are above Cosmic Law. What happens to this planet now is not only in the hands of humanity, but because this is the lone place where we can exist at this moment in time, we help ourselves, humanity, and at the same time we aid the planet, by outflowing unqualified Love and Forgiveness.

Phil Murray
Who are you?

A Silent Knight
A Silent Knight ... to say more would mean I am not a Silent Knight. The exoteric work I accomplish with you means that my anonymous activities are borderline as it is.

Phil Murray
Do you feel that an individual, manifesting these qualities of Love and Forgiveness, makes a real contribution towards a speedier evolutionary process?

A Silent Knight
If you can accept with understanding that our present state began with erroneous and unloving thinking, with consequent behaviour which itself stems from thought first, then it follows that any individual who practices focusing on these thought-forms is reversing the trend, however small a single effect which may be achieved. If such a person were the only one doing it, little would be attained, but SKs and their allies are legion today ... millions, perhaps billions sending out love and forgiveness, radiating the powerful transmutation of the negative fields in which we are immersed. The unexplained changes of certain areas, the Northern Ireland challenge for peace, the Berlin Wall, the fall of Communism, the recognition of Human Rights ... *an idea which is spreading,* are weak starts, but if all of us become SKs we could quickly achieve that well known phrase ON EARTH AS IT IS IN HEAVEN. Most just cannot believe that their thinking has any impact on global problems.

Phil Murray
If you could change one human idiosyncrasy which currently permeates the universal human thought process, what would it be?

A Silent Knight
How I wish the bulk of humanity could simply realize the power of thought-forms and be vigilant of what they say, think and believe ... *belief is focused attention ... attention is the life of thought forms.*

I honestly think that the greater part of humanity wants to live in peace and harmony, but does not understand the great power which could be contributed to its attainment by meditating on the higher goals utilising *good thought-forms*. We all know that *one candle can overcome many times its volume of darkness*. One SKs activity can overcome a thousand times the volume, or *number of people,* of those practising destructive thoughts.

Phil Murray
How can we all live a regular life whilst practising the Silent Knight philosophy?

A Silent Knight
According to the phase of life we inhabit, our attention has to be focused on surviving in the material world as it is. This is for our growth, experiencing, and, maybe this is new to some, *expansion of the Creator's Awareness*. We are the earth-probes so to speak, from the finer planes whose beings cannot stay long in this gross plane any more than our bodies can survive space or deep-sea for very long, without temporary life support systems. But SK philosophy and practice can be done by anyone in idle moments, perhaps when we are letting our thoughts wander. Some may only be able to contribute a few minutes while they go to sleep, or brush their teeth, relieve themselves, whatever. It all adds into the giant flow of the light workers, world servers, and those who render prayers, decrees, and invocations.

I have to mention, whether you wish to include it or not, what was impressed upon me by a teacher to whom I listen. Many seem to have the idea that we only personally develop when we are thinking, meditating, or acting spiritually; I also know many who believe they have personally developed when they get promoted at work, buy a new house or car and perhaps cut a deal they wanted but the other person didn't ... I am not approaching your questions from that angle however ... the important element in all that we say, think and do, is harmony and *harmoniousness*.

Thinking, behaving, living in harmony with the laws of the Creator or Creators, every act in every moment of our lives is an opportunity to remain in harmony with THE PLAN FOR HEAVEN ON EARTH. Therein lies the simple definition of right and wrong, good and evil. We don't have to be taught whether or not we are living harmoniously. That is *a priori* in all of us, even if we try to fool ourselves and others about it.

Phil Murray
Thank you ...

A Silent Knight
Although you didn't ask it, I'd like to give some reasons why SKs remain silent and anonymous, besides those rationalisms which form part of the basic Silent Knight definition. When you embark on this activity and really get into it, you may begin having spooky experiences, as I have mentioned to you during our working together on your books; too many to be mere coincidences! I have said that when you are meditating on Love and Forgiveness ... to repeat myself ... YOU ARE WORKING SHOULDER TO SHOULDER WITH THOSE ASCENDED BEINGS WHO ARE DEDICATED TO THE EVOLUTION OF HUMAN CONSCIOUSNESS. Now if you stay in that company very long, you are bound to be in touch with higher plane conditions to the extent that some super human powers and abilities begin to develop. Imagine now, what would happen if a person actually developed to the ability of an Avatar or a Christ, and this became known to the public. Can you see the tabloids, news media and TV camera crews invading the area, not to mention the constant haranguing and testing by those who were sceptical. The end of all useful spiritual work would be the net result of that unfortunate exercise! The SK or equivalent, would be so harassed and subjected to interviews, possibly with adoring *believers,* he'd get little done spiritually. Then of course there is something about

adulation and attention of the public that can become addictive to us humans. When it becomes delightful, getting attention to a greater extent than a President or a Rock Star for example, few of us would be able to resist the pull back into the material activities of this plane. Only giant beings like Jesus, Krishna, Buddha or Mohammed could prevail against it. I said there is an arcane reason to remain silent about these activities. I hope I have made it clearer now. Remember ... you may have an embodied Angel or Master working beside you and you would not be able to recognize such. He or she would deliberately cover the activity. I hope you know that I have a long way to go before that state prevails for me however, but I prefer that others know nothing about my activities for the above reasons. I am still quite weak against the pull of material world delights.

Always to the best of my ability sending to you, yours and the whole planet ... *Love and Forgiveness* ...

I AM ... *a Silent Knight*

A Silent Knight is anonymous

SMILE

In The Mind Garden of the Microsoft Network on the Internet, I often encounter inspirational and motivational phrases, poems and an assortment of viewpoints. One such instance that recently caught my attention, is a quote from a person called *Maya Angelou*, which read ... *If you have only one smile in you, give it to the people you love.* This is a pleasant enough sentiment, evidently senior to scowling at those who surround you, but I could not help considering climbing further up the ladder of potential by suggesting an alternative, which I submitted as ... *If you have only one smile in you, give it to the people you don't yet love.*

Doing this made me smile with satisfaction! A simple occult maxim is that, *attention given to anything strengthens it*. One of the most difficult tests we can ever encounter is that ability to forgive the apparently unforgivable. The two most moving instances which immediately come to mind when I think about this idea, involves people in Northern Ireland. I remember the father of a bomb victim interviewed on national television news, making no criticism of the terrorist killers and announcing to viewers his total and unconditional forgiveness of those responsible for the death of his daughter. This is living the talk in a big way! The other most recent instance involved the father of an executed taxi driver who forgave the executioner on television.

We must allow our most difficult, unwanted and uninvited, even evil episodes of life, to literally pass straight through us, in order for them to dissolve into the ether waves of eternity, thereby rendered harmless and ineffectual. Any action, thought or verbalisation, which either sanctions or opposes evil, gives strength to it. Yet human nature currently stimulates us to oppose, fight and discuss the evil which occasionally requires attention from us. *Best just let it be,* is the juncture on which I find myself sitting, until a more suitable approach evolves, or evil diminishes to the degree that it does not demand so much attention from us.

Genuine smiling is our unique way of letting things be, allowing others to be, exhibiting satisfaction and exercising more facial muscles than scowling ever can. It is easy and has another advantage in that it produces a physiological reaction of well being, even when forced by an individual. Smiling at hatred without sarcasm or cant, renders the object of your smile less evil and more good. You will have performed a service for both subject and object! *Smile though your heart is aching* adequately sums up another way of making it ache less. *Smile and the world smiles with you* is an optimistic aphorism, with potential never the less. *Smile and your cares fade away,* is a sentiment I enjoy transmitting from time to time. *Smile for no reason at all,* is my favourite.

Writing like this leaves me wide open to being interpreted as encouraging all readers to walk around gaumlessly smiling to everything at inopportune times, frightening little children, and inviting close scrutiny from those qualified to certify you insane. It is better to be known as a smiler than a scowler, I am sure you agree. All I urge in this bite is for us all to smile whenever possible, then a bit more, and when you feel there is nothing to smile about, that is the absolute best time to smile for maximum selfish and altruistic gain ... go on go on go on go on, smile smile smile!

SPECIAL OFFERS

There are not many practical tips in this book are there? A definite absence of popular jargon and extremist vernacular along with little direction, don't you agree? Where are the fun games and exercises where grown, intelligent and responsible business executives get to behave like children who have been refused their toys for too long? How about noticing that there is no reference to gaining advantage over fellow humanity for a quick sale?

Special offers usually arrive with nothing special in them, with one constant exception! Invariably this is my experience. I am all too aware of transmitting useless beliefs either wittingly or otherwise, to readers who may take at face value all that I write. I would be just as pleased if you assimilated no data whatsoever from this work, hopefully substituting that book norm for a self impregnation of inspiration.

When I began life as a performer in the North East Clubs of England, I remember a friend of mine called Alan ran a comedy show group called Pyramid. One night in the Sands Club, Whitley

Bay, I witnessed his performance which was undoubtedly hilarious. He opened the second act dressed as a vicious, racist skin head. Remember that quaint and thankfully transient shave your head fashion of the early nineteen seventies; dressing and presenting your body to look horrible, provoking fear in everyone including your grandmother!

Holding a bass guitar which seemed twice the size of its player, Alan barked out the new lyrics which he had written to the old melody of Pick A Bale Of Cotton. *Oh lawdy!* They went something like this ... *I'm gonna jump down turn around knack a Pakistani gonna jump down turn around knack a Pak a day; oh lawdy, knack a Pakistani, oh lawdy knack a Pak a day!*

As you may have guessed, the song was satire aimed at instigators of this silly skinhead movement which deemed the action of Paki-bashing, beating up those who looked like they originated from the general direction of Asia, nationally advantageous and personally stimulating. The trouble with Alan's act was that it unintentionally provoked the audience into a chorus of agreement that Paki-bashing was okay. He dropped the song and we lost another opportunity for inspiration through the humour of an artist.

The audience were all too willing to be carried along unthinkingly onto the path of least resistance. Some walked out of the show as a demonstration of solidarity with their brothers and sisters, and this latter action was almost as bad as the former described.

I remember a telephone call regarding possible membership of the Positive Attitude Club. The caller requested me to describe what kind of followers I had. No kind, I replied quickly, not wishing to offend, but willing to if need be, as an effort to disillusion this person from an outlook on the PAC as far from reality as one may get. It would be mentally easier for many to join the PAC if an enrolee was able to follow the pattern of group thought established by earlier members. There is no such group thought however, no extreme viewpoints and no special offers. We have a forum and that is all. Some people come, only to tell me that it isn't very good ... I ask them why *they* didn't make it very good. I have heard particular evenings described as not as good as the last one. Yet, the last one belonged to that person just as the latest one did!

It is so easy to sit back and be the audience, but contribution is so much more worthwhile. Some assail their way to the top whilst others violate their way to the bottom. A balance in life is ever the most beneficial for all aspects, and *gradual graduation* is the rule in all change that we contemplate.

Many people spend their lives searching out special offers in an effort to get more than they should for their money, whilst others spend breathing time creating special offers for those followers to spend their money on.

Life is *the* special offer my friend, and yours exists for you to create, or have created for you. This special offer is the one constant exception to which I previously alluded. The special offer of life always comes with something extra special in it! Those who would create it for you are having a bit of your special offer for free at no risk to themselves. Those who create life inspiringly for themselves are the greatest artists this earth has yet to produce.

To partake of this special offer all you need do is begin the creation of your life as the most precious commodity you will ever own. Discover your own unique story which is you, and tell that story through living. Demonstrate who you are with sensitive thought and aesthetic action. Begin to *be* ... just BE.

SPEED LIMITS

Why make a population feel guilty, by setting an unrealistically low speed limit on the roads, resulting in more driver's attention being devoted to the rear view mirror and potential traps than on safety? Superficially, you may feel that this is not relevant to a personal development book; I think it is.

I am also well aware of the dichotic nature of reader's viewpoints on such subjects. I hear wails from Friends of the Earth armies crying ban the car altogether. I feel nature lovers all over, singing the song to halt all technical progress. Public transport devotees enthuse about the environmental benefits of municipal trains, planes, boats and buses ... why is it that I ponder the concept of car ownership for all?

I understand the dulling nature of suppression!

Ultimately, you will not ever discourage any population from a natural urge, an exciting trend, or a helpful service. Sure, you can impose artificial will on the masses by banning religion, like the former Soviet Union, by announcing that there is no God. A country can show its moral stance by prohibiting marijuana, and have the users do shady deals in underground car parks with often tragic results. You must know of families who refuse to bless the sexual relationship of a son or daughter, only to have them exhibit their natural yearnings elsewhere, and confiding in others the confession of pregnancy or sexually transmitted disease.

We can work, as I choose, with Evolution, against it, or a compromise of both possibilities!

As an audio producer, I encountered the owner of a large talking book catalogue who was interested in me recording some books for him. When I proudly announced that my recording facility was digital, he promptly withdrew his interest. He believed that digital recording was not necessary, along with compact discs. He spoke diatribes about the benefits of vinyl records and $^1/_4$ inch analogue tape, whilst castigating my digital equipment to the universal scrap heap of bad ideas. He has since purchased a digital audio tape recorder and two compact disc writers ... it was not possible to progress in the industry without being able to communicate, using relevant mediums, to his business contemporaries.

I live in the countryside surrounding London, yet in between the fields of sheep, rapeseed and fallow, snarl lines of congested, wheezing roads, full of private cars as eager to get off them as are the environmentalists to get them off. I wrote a letter to my local newspaper suggesting that we make one offending road narrower, with an abundance of pedestrian crossing points, thus encouraging motorists to use other roads and annoy people elsewhere. The sardonic wit was ignored and the letter printed, as an alternative to the witterings of the *by-pass now* brigade.

The point is this ... we can fight the urges of a population, or, when legitimate and ethical, work with them as co-operation with evolution. A metaphor involving aikido, where the opponents energy is utilised in your own favour is relevant at this point. The futility of tirades about the evil computer age is nagging and suppressive. The fear concerning a World Wide Web of Internet users, communicating in a world forum of philosophy, is sad. The media writes about the so called epidemic of pornography *on the net*, when the real fear is exuded from further up the control ladder, and is connected to freedom of the masses to speak about anything, to anyone willing to flick the switch of a computer and dial a number using a modem.

We are living in a world of lightning quick advances and progress. Not all will be to everyone's liking, but the minute that suppression of any kind is utilised to control such advance, is also the time when the introduction of more laws signal the advent of further fear, and a society slipping over on its own aspirations.

I honestly believe that a happy future lies with the exploration in a *pan awareness* of all aspects connected to every societal and industrial advance we make. This translates into road users co-operating with environmentalists in a win for all strategy, perhaps culminating in fresh forests being created alongside new roads. If people want cars, and let's face it they are the most convenient mode of transport available to us, having accomplished more for physical human freedom than any one individual viewpoint has, no matter how alternative and inspirational, then let us work on ways of providing cars and roads, whilst enhancing the environment and improving the quality of life for the whole planet. It *can* be done. We must first join in positive thought that such splendid co-operative endeavour is not only possible, but essential.

Every punitive and unrealistic speed limit that is imposed, results in masses of guilt when people find themselves unable to comply. We must be realistic about such laws and understand the effect constant misdemeanour has upon the individual psyche. All that I here write is but an exoteric rendition of something far more esoteric which is sweeping the universe at this present time. Civilisation is more creative now that at any other time in known history. We must go with the flow and impulse of such creativity, and importantly note that we have a duty to avoid stifling it in any way, shape or form.

The sooner we create our own speed limits is the earlier we enjoy our own personal government. Rule from within! Inside your own universe is the only place you can truly commune with nature. You esoterically invent your own rules or not, as your karmic case may be. You thereafter communicate exoterically with fellow humanity using a deeper understanding of human creativity in all its splendour, and with all its subjective shortcomings.

The turmoil that you can visibly see, is a direct reflection of the invisible which is busy inside our collective inner beings. It is time to release the personal development brakes and let ourselves go ... full speed ahead Mr Bosun ... full speed ahead!

SPONTANEOUS DISCUSSION

And so we held a Positive Attitude Club evening around the subject of SPONTANEOUS DISCUSSION. Very cleverly and quite unspontaneously, I decided to prepare for this discussion by defining the word spontaneous using the dictionary. Now, those readers who have experienced a PAC(K) will know that the subject for any evening is merely a stimulus to explore anything interesting which may float our way. This subject however, was particularly attractive to me, as I believed that it formed the basis of any successful human interplay.

After mooching around a few varying definitions, I pieced one together with which I was comfortable ... *self origination arising without external cause.*

An exciting concept was unfolding; if being spontaneous meant hatching something brand new from within, without external stimuli, then that would surely bypass all tired and worn paradigms already in place, which may have outlasted their usefulness. Those who had arrived for an evening of spontaneous chit chat about their journey to the PAC and the state of British weather, quickly adapted to this approach, as we began discussing just what a paradigm is ... *a mental map ... a way of viewing the world ... a method of perception.*

The map is not the territory of course, it is merely the box of illusions through which we always filter our surroundings. The mental map can be thought of as that material which precedes the formation of our viewpoint. I suggested that we all change one viewpoint for the better during our two hours together, and this was agreed as a good idea, although we did not ask for confirmation that everyone had accomplished this task ... that would remain a private part of each individual's process, according to PAC principles.

As a writer, I was interested in the exploration of inspiration, and The Storyteller had mentioned a kind of invocation as being the only spontaneity humans are currently capable of achieving. He then drew our attention to the derivation of the word spontaneous ... some latecomers questioned the necessity of delving into too much detail, but agreement was forthcoming ... we decided to continue, and after consideration, all comers were happy with this procedure.

The Storyteller, who had also quite unspontaneously utilised a reference in the Madame Blavatsky book *Isis Unveiled* as preparation for his contribution to the evening, mentioned the Greek derivation as being from the word *ponein,* which means *to toil* ... he continued by describing the aim of many Greek Mystery Schools as being a working towards *Soul Contact*. That brought us to the subject of spontaneous human combustion perhaps occurring because of soul contact being achieved without the necessary preparation. Attendees of these schools were expected to allow their first two years of membership to pass in silence. It seems they were serious about their aspirations!

Now, I am aware that BEFORE THE BEGINNING IS A THOUGHT, but I was interested to explore *that spark* which occurs just before the thought. Is this the inspirational invocation to which The Storyteller was alluding ... is this plugging into The Ether Waves, which I describe in YOU CAN ALWAYS GET WHAT YOU WANT ... is this an awareness of the universal life force of which we are all an intrinsic part?

We could only discuss briefly, these concepts which are in fact fundamental mysteries to many of us. I telephoned The Storyteller on the following day, and he reminded me of how we all sought linear solutions to these logical questions. What about the holistic approach to such answers?

When I meditate, I feel closest to just being. It is a wonderful experience of nothing ... for me that is. If I was able to hold my beingness in this state during the hustle bustle of everyday life, then I truly feel that an aspiration I keep with me at all times to *be more me*, would be fulfilled.

Spontaneity is soul contact; this cannot be rushed, and if called upon too soon can ruin an individuals chance of further soul recognition for much time to come. Seek it by all means; of course I encourage such action, but remember that you may be contacting something as spontaneous as the creation of a universe ... and so the chat went ...

SPOT CARPENTER THE FISH MAN

"That's a nice new van Spot," noticed Edith Sullivan, one of Spot's oldest customers, "how d'you afford that then hinny; charging us pensioners too much for Hake I'll bet!" Edith smiled a challenging glance at her friendly fish merchant, who knew better than to correct her, regardless of the wanting accuracy concerning Edith's observations.

"Nice piece of Faeroe Cod this morning Edith, or some fresh Lemon Sole off the Dogger Bank," replied Spot without reference to her allegation, "I'd recommend the Halibut, but I know better pet

... you've never had it in the 30 years you've been buying from me!"

Spot wrapped her the smallest Cod fillet he was carrying, and she slapped his van on the side in acknowledgement, before walking back home over the lane, stockings rolled around ankles. This stimulated Spot into a fresh bout of admiration for the sign writing with which his new white vehicle was adorned ... SPOT CARPENTER THE FISH MAN, was blazed in bright blues, greens and yellows, running the full length of his van. He had a quick thought about his retirement, but stifled it before the thought could take hold.

It was quiet, even though he was parked in that buoyant commercial spot which he had frequented all his professional life, and the youthful existence previous to it, as a lad with an eye for the trawlers. Well known in that area of North Shields which overlooked the River Tyne Fish Quay, times were changing fast, and Spot had not kept abreast of the fearsome transformation. He was 64 years old, and his business had leaned with the seasons for 50 of them. He began with a barrow, selling the leftovers from the 5am market, and there he was still, retirement age dawning, and a computer oriented generation of new blood reliant heavily on American imported fashionable fast foods, television advertised as *the* things to eat, had left him with a dwindling asset and an outmoded pride, resulting in the recent and paradoxical purchase of his relatively superfluous new van.

"Got any kippers kidda," asked a young lad in a hurry, "I just fancy some for me tea tonight."

"You'll have to keep fancying for another three months son, because I only sell freshly smoked mackerel; they're out of season, so will you have a piece of Rock instead?" was Spot's authoritative and suggestive reply to the young lad he recognised from the Mr

Whippy ice cream factory over the road, which was still up for sale after two and a half years on the market.

"Got none frozen then?" continued the young lad hopefully.

"Sunbeam, I'm not a supermarket; I'm Spot Carpenter the mobile fish man," corrected the wounded pride of a life's dedication to the commercial exploitation of our marine life.

"You'll not get rich with that attitude," insisted the young lad, "you've got to give the customers what they want these days."

"Aye lad, and what happens if what they want is not as good as I can give them," asked Spot rising to the bait, "what does your youthful intelligence say to that?"

"It says change," responded the young lad beginning with a respect which grew weary, "but I know you'll not do that. I can tell. I get the feeling you're just about to launch into a verbal rendition of thoughts currently circulating your brain describing the good old days," he pointed down to the quay which held fast the ropes of precious few fishing boats, "you're going to tell me all about the halcyon days of those great trawler companies like Irving and Purdy, who had no necessity for concession to commercial pressures, because they dictated the pace of everything connected with fish. You're itching to tell me all about good old fashioned manners, real English ice cream, pre-decimalisation money, your Dad who was a deck hand on the George V tug boat, a pint of beer from the barrel, your uncle who steered the pilot boat with a Latin name, and the good old sing songs you all had around the back of the smoke house down Tanners Bank."

Spot listened with patience and a swelling interest, as his frown uncreased and the lad continued.

"While the world gears up for real progress, immaculate hygiene, fast everything whenever you want it, new roads, new housing, clever development, exploitation of the new markets in China, Africa, the Middle East and South America, you're going to stand here day after day shouting *fish*, while everybody who used to support you is round the corner at the new hypermarket buying seafood caught by Australians in the South Pacific, irradiated to safety and devoid of any chance of food poisoning!"

Spot's patience held out as his interest decreased, "I see what you are saying kidda, and I think you are right. Just because I'm a fish man doesn't mean I'm thick you know. Those long cold Tuesday mornings spent standing here in the rain were handy for thinking, but those thoughts never seemed to take me anywhere. 50 years pass by and you come along; a slip of a lad barely out of nappies. But you see, my secret weapon has always been this ... to learn from everyone and everything! Now, when you started talking my first impulse was to kick your arse into the river, but I fought that instinct and looked for the good in what you were saying. There wasn't any, so I looked a bit further and realised that even though there was an absence of good, you were right never the less. The world is progressing just as you have said, and I am not advancing in the same way. So, I am going to put that right today!"

"What, you're going to buy a refrigeration unit just because of what I've just said," asked the lad with vanity and mock amazement.

"I'm not," corrected Spot, "I'm going to put in an offer on that ice cream factory you work in. I've always secretly fancied it, and I even made enquiries when it was first up for sale ... it'll be much cheaper now, and this new van of mine will be kitted out as the new SPOT CARPENTER'S MR WHIPPY MOBILE ICE CREAM EXTRAVAGANZA."

The lad was astounded. He composed himself whilst staring into space towards a new generation oil platform, lethargically making way down the river and out towards the fields off Aberdeen. With a smile, he risked a question, "what about my job then, is it safe?"

"Which department are you in son," asked Spot in reply, as a middle aged lady customer joined them.

"Accounts," was the muffled reply.

"Well," continued Spot, "the job's safe, but you won't be in it. I reckon I have proved myself in your department by saving up enough money over the years to buy the firm you work for ... you can prove yourself by working SPOT CARPENTER'S MR WHIPPY MOBILE ICE CREAM EXTRAVAGANZA ... if you want that is kidda?"

"And I thought I'd done you a favour," said the lad as he turned and walked back over to the factory head bowed low, "this is what I get for me efforts."

"You did me a favour son," concluded Spot as the lad kept walking, "but that was not what you intended. It was me who looked for the good in what you were saying by sticking to my working class philosophy of always seeking an education in everything that comes my way. I'm not soft though but. You don't think I'd want a smart arse like you kicking round my heels for the rest of my days ... I'm not totally vindictive so I offered you something that would keep you out of my sight for most of the time. Now that you are resentful of that concession you better start looking for another job because you're sacked the minute I take over."

The lad was stunned. His walk transformed into a trot and he disappeared behind the factory gates

"Modern day commercial pressures me old son," shouted Spot tauntingly after the lad, "you should know all about them! *Fish ... fish ... get your fish from Spot.*" Two cats looked on; Spot untied his apron and stuffed it into the public bin to which he always parked adjacent. The middle aged lady who had patiently waited with interest eventually spoke ...

"Is that right Spot," she asked naively, "are you taking over the ice cream factory?"

"D'you think I'm divvy pet ... d'you think I'm tuppence short of a bob ... here," he showed her his last box of young codling, "take what you like for nowt and give the rest to those cats, I've just retired early. I couldn't tell him that though but ... he would have had to show me how to do it properly!"

STITCH IN TIME

On Thursday, the 23rd May 1996 at 08.30, a child was knocked down by a car on the Crawley Down Road, whilst crossing towards Felbridge County Primary School in Surrey, where she was a pupil. I called an ambulance, it arrived and whisked her off to hospital where I knew she would be well cared for. Thankfully, the injury amounted to bruising, but as I listened to the chat of parents as they arrived and witnessed what was happening, the sentiment was unanimous ... *one of these days a child will be killed and then we will get the assisted crossings we have requested for so long!*

Of course it is plain to understand that nobody actually wants to have a child killed, in order for the remainder to live more safely, so why does this phenomenon of turning a blind eye to the obvious persist? I have my own personal feelings about that answer, but they will do little in the short term to accelerate the installation of a pedestrian crossing over the A264 between Mill Lane, Felbridge, and its junction with the Crawley Down Road; and another over the Crawley Down Road, close to the actual school itself. *My thoughts on the subject turned cosmic,* but I concentrated on the challenge at hand ... I wrote to the local newspapers ...

> Perhaps an open invitation to the powers that be would help: Try crossing the A264 in the described vicinity, between 08.00 and 09.00 hours, or any other time for that matter, and see how you feel about road safety after your experience. Then, picture yourself as one of many children who try this daily!
>
> We look forward to effective action from those responsible at their earliest opportunity. Meanwhile, to motorists and pedestrians alike ... beware of the dangers which exist in this area ... no one wants to be caught up in the hideous atmosphere of an accident!
>
> With positive thoughts of effective action ...
>
> Phil Murray ... leader of the PAC

The newspapers telephoned me back in response to my faxes, but they were merely interested in the incident from a gossip angle. I had a material vested interest too; I made those dangerous crossings daily with my daughter, and up until 1995 had done so also with my son. In that same area I had also been the victim of what is now described tabloid fashion, as *road rage* ... this is where other motorists insult you, or worse, aware only of their own circumstances and not yours. In my case this amounted to abusive language from another driver, far worse of which I had been known to utilise myself in earlier days.

My power lay in harmlessness however! Not *adding* any rage to the situation! This is an art which I am still learning and perhaps will be for many more incarnations to come. My smile at this fellow motorist angered him more so I had to think of alternatives; I drove on as quickly as possible, this being my considered effective response.

Now, I am a big, strong fellow, and could easily have jumped out of my car and *lamped* the abuser, to utilise the vernacular. My vocabulary is vast, but my colloquial knowledge of contemporary insults would have floored him even without it ... the Geordie accent helps with the fear angle it seems, and I have been known to use it, I must say. That was a long time ago and all part of my own personal learning and growing process. I do not use physical violence yet I could. I do not shout harmful words yet I could. I do not gossip yet I could. I do not follow group opinion yet I could. These *nots* are tiring me out!

What should I be conveying to you?

My intention is that I constantly improve in every way ... every day. This is an affirmation of mine ...

> every day in every way
> in all I do and all I say
> I pledge myself to this intent
> a life of love wisely spent

So, I turn these *disasters* into *successes*. This is another method I employ whenever something less than resourceful happens. Unfortunate incidents are turned into lessons and stories for myself as well as those wishing to share my travels. Most users of the A264 would like traffic to travel more quickly on it ... yet the villagers in Felbridge want it to slow down ... the *road rager* wants to let of steam at another fellow ... I prefer listening to the speeches of Winston Churchill. This universe is filled with dichotomies, and one mode of learning the cosmic ways is called *Harmony Through Conflict*.

This planet is filled with conflict of all types; hurricanes destroying otherwise harmonious areas of development, to produce the clichéd calm after the storm; rivalry of the second world war resulting in a stronger and more harmonious Europe; forest fires which are the harbingers of plants that can only grow after such disaster; pondering opposing human thought which results in cognition ... *the sudden dawning of a new reality*; and you in general, going through human existence, killing so much life with each step you take, mouthful you eat, flask you drink, house you build, road you plan, and idea you suppress. From such waste, bountiful harmony must surely arise. It is our duty to ensure that it does. For without the inspiration which follows each low, we would not evolve according to The Plan. Just because that Plan may well be perfect, is not an excuse for you to let it run a course without adding your contribution to the reservoir of human endeavour.

A stitch in time may well save nine, but the experience is in the holistic picture ... however you interpret it!

STORYTELLING AND PERSONAL DEVELOPMENT
an interview with The Storyteller

Phil Murray
What impact do your stories have with an individual's onward progress?

The Storyteller
Your question probably relates to The Storyteller's trilogy of audio cassette tape programmes. What I aim for with these programmes is to show that we can look at our lives as an adventure ... from wherever we start, our lives are full of possibilities to gain insights and deeper understanding of that mysterious thing called life. *Take life as it is and then make something special out of it,* is my belief.

Phil Murray

I know that you have also given lectures during your life; why do you prefer the storytelling method of disseminating what seems to be material having a similar aim as that contained within your lectures?

The Storyteller

As a lecturer the impression is created that I know it all. My words in themselves are a *fait accompli.* In storytelling, we create a participatory feeling of exploration. As a lecturer it is about what I know. As a storyteller it is about who we are. As a lecturer the illusion is created of those who know and of those who do not know. As a storyteller we become *one* in the *universal story.*

Phil Murray

Who are you?

The Storyteller

I am a story ... an unfolding story ... so I have no specific boundaries that restrict *what* I am. Every turn of life's pages, stories reveal themselves, and as a person that people call *The Storyteller* ... I share. When we open ourselves to the remembering of the past, the diversity of the present and the eternity of the future, there is little need for an *I*. To be a person is to have a story to tell.

Phil Murray

Do you feel that any of us can make a real contribution towards a more happy evolutionary process?

The Storyteller

Phil ... having pondered this question along with the following two questions, in order to respond to them from the viewpoint of a storyteller ... *as a story rather than an answer,* in other words ... I feel the following human stories relate closely to your three questions. From my point of view they are not real questions to the storyteller, but are more relevant to the lecturer ... the first story tells of a humanity in harmony with nature. At one with nature. In this first story humanity worships nature and centres every aspect of its life around the sacredness of nature. This humanity delivers itself into the hands of nature, willingly sacrificing its most precious belongings to win nature's favour and protection; celebrating in nature's abundance and living by nature's passions.

Phil Murray
If you could change one human trait which currently permeates the generic human thought process, what would it be?

The Storyteller
This story tells of a humanity with complete dominion over nature. This humanity, convinced that it has a divine mandate to rule over every living and none living thing on earth, makes domination its passion. Nature is its enemy, something to be subdued, managed, tamed and conquered. This humanity takes nature into its own hands, wilfully stripping the earth bare in an effort to make nature predictable, law abiding and efficiently productive.

Phil Murray
How can we all learn to live our own personal stories more accurately, and with less influence from external stimuli?

The Storyteller
This third story tells of a humanity existing alongside nature, neither immersed in it nor concerned with domination over it. This humanity knows that everything existing in this world is simply illusion; an effect of some invisible cause, a reflex from some intangible stimulation of matter. This humanity empties its hands of nature, willingly ignoring nature as a means to reap supernatural rewards. Free from all worldly bounds. As a storyteller I wonder ... *is it time for a fourth story?*

Phil Murray
Thank you ...

The Storyteller is Nico Thelman

TAKE A BREAK AND RECREATE

No matter what we contemplate, whether it be a positive action or indeed a negative deed, helpful to the planet or an eternal hindrance, life enhancing or spiritually destructive, the clever amongst us will always adopt a positive mental attitude towards both our intention, and action, if we are to be ultimately successful.

Life is a succession of experiences, which we will be able to utilise for our personal development if we are aware of such opportunity, or conversely, a procession of expired happenings which have used us, depending on our frame of mind.

I founded The Positive Attitude Club, often known as *the PAC(K),* because I believe in the importance of a positive frame of mind in all we think and do. We have the choice ... we are the only known species who can think about how we think ... we can look at the way we look at the world ... most importantly, we can change our circumstances by thought and thought alone. No finance is needed for this venture, no particular habitat, no other people of like mind; just you utilising the power of your mind!

There is not one person amongst us who does not wish to alter some aspect of personal life for the better. Whether it is a *you to you,* a *you to others,* an *others to you* or an *others to others* change, makes no difference ... to execute such modification requires creative thought, and this type of thought mainly requires silence, stillness, solitude and determination, if it is to be effective. I have called this situation which I feel we must all seek regularly, *Time To Myself,* in all of my preceding books, and shortened this title to TTM, which is nice and easy to remember. What we really need however, is something nice and easy which reminds us to remember TTM!

Now, many of us work hard at a variety of life's tasks, and hard workers during leisure time are frequently seen on the squash courts, swimming a few lengths of the local pool, jogging, playing on computers, gardening, drinking alcohol or eating meals in fancy restaurants. Fine! There is certainly many varying activities to suit the diversity of human beings which we definitely are.

But this is not recreation in its truest sense!

Re-creation ... this word implies some kind of change does it not? It alludes to a fundamental modification of the modus operandi with which it is identified. I invite you to consider an extra dimension to your world of recreation; as for its importance, this is for you to decide.

Most of us have been burdened by a socialisation process not in harmony with our present situations. Children up until recently, and even now new attitudes are in the minority, have been suffered as present time problems rather than future planetary assets. In accordance with their status, little time was afforded to their soul growth as they were bundled through family life, a weak school system still unaware of the main definition of education, which is to *learn from within,* and onwards to the job world. If any piece of a personal story, purpose or true raison d'être lived through these shocks, they were the exceptions rather than the majority.

Further anomalies exist in our appraisal of the human condition. We can find brilliant people in one aspect of life, who are lousy human beings in the main. The socialisation process does not separate true achievement *as a spirit having a human experience* with those who consider themselves *humans experiencing an occasional spiritual enlightenment.* So, we find singularly powerful executives, controlling many of us who have achieved a more *pan determined* viewpoint of life. They appear to be higher on the scale of human endeavour, yet many have not even made it to the first rung of the PAC Ladder, which leads to real elevation of a cosmic nature.

So, these people play around with powerful toys, unaware of their responsibility to those intrinsically far more powerful than themselves, and an uncomfortable and idiosyncratic socialisation process continues into adult life!

You will frequently find yourself in circumstances where you are more spiritually aware than those who execute a degree of control over you. The most enlightened of us do not blatantly draw attention to these situations without due care and attention; rather, a *living the talk* response is far more relevant to any *sabre rattling* impulse you may find rising in you. We all need to *take a break and recreate;* those who do not understand the process even more so than those of us who do understand it. It is those of us who do understand such need however, who must lead the way by example, and such example must be seen as *living the talk* in both attitude and action.

Your recreation must include TTM if it is to lead you onward and ever upward. Of course the similarities between TTM, prayer, meditation and contemplation exist. I have not invented anything new here. I only *re-present* ageless wisdom in a particular way that attracts people who would not necessarily be drawn to such a body of knowledge in its purest form, which this is most definitely not, although quite workable and agreeable in its own right.

Find a convenient and peaceful place where you are comfortable to be alone with yourself. Close your eyes and get acquainted with your inner world. Note any stray thoughts which pass your way, and work at this TTM idea until you are able to maintain a state of *thoughtlessness*. Then, from your daily life, retrieve one situation, set of circumstances or attitude, which you would like to change, develop, understand more thoroughly, or merely contemplate. Place as much attention as you can muster onto this process and encourage the conclusion you wish to have.

Creation in mental matter is the direct precursor of its more solidly physical equivalent. If you get it right in the mental universe, natural law states quite categorically that physical manifestation must correspondingly occur. Does it not make sense then to utilise your recreation time for the design of your life exactly as you wish it to be?

I think so! I therefore urge you to take a break and recreate ...

TASTE

In the summer of 1993, I completed my trilogy of *solo* music albums. The project was a joint venture between my publishing and recording company, and another entertainment oriented company in the west end of London. Although I produced the album from an artistic angle, a condition of the deal was that the owner of the partnership company would executively produce the project. This *executive producer* title means in general, the organising of finance and studio time, together with any other logistical arrangements that the programme requires.

With each consecutive album, I had gradually introduced an increased focus towards backing vocals, and on the one we are discussing, which is called FOREVER AGAIN, I decided, in the pursuit of a personal quality which I was expressing musically, to administer some serious *alternative* notes into the harmonic arrangements. After completing the recording of a song called NATURALLY, the executive producer entered the studio, wincing at some unseen pain which was obviously permeating his personal universe.

Are you going to repair it, he asked.

I knew he was referring to a sixth note which I had included right at the end of the song, which *was* open to varied interpretation.

I think the notes work well, I responded.

But they are wrong, he continued.

They are not wrong, I concluded, *they are just not to your taste!*

As I was indeed the artistic operator in this instance, the note remained and the album was released to coincide unfortunately, with the release of YOU CAN ALWAYS GET WHAT YOU WANT as a single audio cassette tape programme. We placed all of our promotion endeavours into the latter, which is still successful as I write these words in 1997, and the former fell by the wayside *for the time being*. Much bad feeling was forthcoming from the executive producer however, before the matter paled into inevitable insignificance, and it all happened because of indistinction between two concepts ... *taste* and *quality*.

If you travel a lifetime of misunderstanding, forever confusing taste with quality, you will render yourself far less effectual than would otherwise be the case were you to make the necessary distinction between these two ideas. How many times do we hear the words ... *I hate that, it's rubbish ... he couldn't sing if his life depended on it ... those cars are skanky!*

Taste is a paradigm ... it is an intrinsic component of your *box of illusions* through which is filtered all that you perceive, into comfortable compartments. It has little or nothing to connect it with actuality. Human beings are blessed with an ability to quickly change any taste they may have formulated, for another; you may also like to alter a particular taste and have no opinion whatsoever for that aspect of life you once had taste about. The permutations for change are endless. Quality is a rightness however, a concept which just *is!*

Right and wrong is a different matter. We may note that the only consummate rightness in this universe is *The Divine Plan* which *is* perfect, no matter how odd and paradoxical that may seem. We may also say that as this plan is perfect, so is the working out of it; this working out of the plan is what we frequently seem to be *enduring* in this business we call life. In other words ... *things are just as they should be* ... to paraphrase a tiny aspect of the Hindu Vedas, in a distinctly Buddhist way. How you relate dreadful aspects of life which are happening all around us every day to this idea of karma, is for individual pondering. These concepts are real to me however, no matter how obscure they may appear in the first instance, to you the reader.

This *things are just as they should be* idea is a supreme vehicle for both laziness and zeal. Which you choose is a matter of evolutionary progress, if indeed you choose either! Bearing *things are just as they should be* in mind, what can we do to improve the human lot? Well of course, human reaction to the plan is all part of it; without world wars we would have less appreciation of peace ... building developers draw more public attention to nature than does any one *friend of the earth* type of organisation, for without the builders there would be no *extra* attention on our natural world. Without discordant music, would it be possible to appreciate harmony in quite the same way?

When looking to contribute over and above to this divine plan I talk about which is apparently perfect, I propose that attention to quality will bear good yields. Personal taste is irrelevant ... it will change with each personality you assume every new lifetime.

Quality will remain as does a hanging note of music drifting into eternity.

If you contribute quality to life, you will soon find little time available for these irrelevant little tastes we all have leftover from a bygone age of outmoded ideas. The quality you contribute into our mutual lives, will not be to everyone's taste of course, and this is a factor which frequently turns people away from a good idea and back into the human rut of public opinion, which is frequently a group of sick and infantile ideas hatched by a silly group of journalists sitting around an editorial desk minutes away from an equally crass publishing deadline.

Which road do you want to travel?

The well worn route which most take because it is easy? The path shown to you by your socialisation process? The way society leans with trends, fads, gimmicks and gizmos? Or will you take the road less well travelled, which is maintained by the few, for the many who inevitably will follow?

I invite you to change any old, unworkable paradigms, and replace them with ... NOTHING! Get naked ... bare all ... expose yourself ... be vulnerable! Erase your opinions until intuition begins to reappear. Decide that your only taste is that of a *pursuit of quality*.

Should I show these words to that executive producer?

TELEPATHY AND PSYCHIC AURAS

The PAC(K) had just finished and a girl approached me to announce that mine was the first aura she had ever seen. Monosyllabicacy is not my speciality; in this case however, as I had not even seen this aura that she mentioned myself, I smiled, uttered *good,* and hoped for an interruption. Weeks later I caught myself with an associate, relating to her an exercise I had undertaken for the previous week, which included visualising herself and a mutual friend prior to my meditations. I got the feeling that there was an expectation of telepathy and quickly added to my rendition, the fact that her awareness of my visualisation was not necessary, and certainly no reflection of any psychic ability.

Just as the old age carries with it expectations of academic studies, climbing the corporate ladder and telling your children not to swear, so too does the new age impinge negatively onto a person susceptible to external pressures pertaining to the increasing of one's telepathic powers, psychic perception and many other potential abilities. This can lead to stress just as can the bank clerk's yearning for the super-stardom of area managership.

A lady called me regarding the book she was writing; *I need someone to put it together for me,* she began, *there are piles of scribbles all around me, with references and newspaper cuttings ...* I uncharacteristically cut her communication with a pertinent question. *Has any of your material been typed into a word processing format, because ..?* She reciprocated my interruption with an anxious one of her own. *I don't believe in them; I believe in miracles and the fact that someone will just take this mess I have created and make it into a best-selling book.* I know this serendipitous feeling she was transmitting, having aspired to experiencing it myself long ago. *Yes,* I responded, *I believe in miracles too, but the particular one of which you are expectant, will require somebody's energy at some point in time to type it!*

She asked me to send her details of my company, preferring not to give out her surname, which she eventually did. *Everybody uses a surname so I don't,* she announced triumphantly, *just as I refuse to begin a letter with "Dear" ... and end it with "Yours Truly."*

And how does this approach help you realise a fulfilled life, was to have been my conclusive question, but it just did not seem to form in the vocal chords. The lips began to shape for delivery, but the tongue did not act, *it fairly clove to the roof of my mouth!*

One set of beliefs become substituted with another, and the wheel goes around and around. *I believe in God now ... I used to like Newcastle United but now I prefer Sunderland ... butter is nice but ghee is better ... I was Labour but now I am Liberal ... I swore like a trooper but now I think it is disgusting ...*

The person who was once proud of an ability to verbally destroy an opponent during the corporate climb, crosses over to the new age and takes the same pride in having to see psychic auras more clearly than any contemporaries. The fervent agnostic becomes the fanatical believer. Where is the difference? I do not see it! Hang ups and crutches with different names. The universe is exactly as it is, whether or not you believe it. Your mental map may read a certain way, but it does not necessarily relate to the territory you are attempting to interpret.

As I have already mentioned earlier in this book, *things are just as they should be;* it approximately states this sentiment somewhere in the Vedas, used by Hindus and others. The word Veda itself is Sanskrit, and means knowledge. Collectively, they are four sacred texts composed between 1800 and 1200 BC. The Rig-Veda, the Sama-Veda, the Yajur-Veda and the Atharva-Veda.

Knowledge is knowledge, not humanly coloured one way or another, as that becomes diluted knowledge, which is an inferior companion. Things are just as they should be, is not an excuse to do nothing about an aspect of life which requires improving, but is intrinsically connected with karma. By all means improve your health and contact with the real you within; this will aid an effective assimilation of data knowledge just as it will help an easier digestion of mystical and intuitive unwordable enlightenment. If you are just replacing old beliefs with new ones however, things are still just as they should be, until you feel they could be better! Then they are still just as they should be!

All the time you are believing in something, you are less sensitive to life. If you try to grow telepathic and psychic powers in a mental hothouse, they will be unnatural, as are the tomatoes grown in England, picked ready for your consumption in May. What are you to do with any new powers and abilities you are aspiring towards anyway. Do you need them for your job? Can you get the feeling that if you lead a healthy life of goodwill and service, certain mystical apparencies may evolve your way regardless.

Unless you are involved with psychic research, telepathic investigation or aura detection as an avocation, or a hobby, then why not place your attention on an evolutionary service which will accelerate naturally the descent of all we aspire towards, onto our prepared plates.

A useful evolutionary service which come to mind also contains massive gains for any who partake of it. It is called *stripping the crap*. This involves the continuous removal of all beliefs, opinions, unnatural aspirations and unwanted socialisations, until you are mentally naked. During this exercise, one may feel regular desires to dress again, perhaps using different clothes. Resist this yearning and place you attention on an external service, like the mental flowing of love and forgiveness into the astral smog which clogs the aura of our planet ... *or hospital visiting?*

Life begins with the cognition that you are life.

TELEVISION TELEPHONE RADIO AND THE INTERNET

This technological age in which we find ourselves living and breathing, is without doubt the most stunning achievement we have as yet accomplished as a thinking race. We truly have the capabilities which allow us to consider ourselves the *mythical,* from that time in the sixties when this phrase was coined, *global village.* We can touch the hearts of millions, by beaming pictures around the planet of starving children in Africa. We can respond to those pictures with concerts simultaneously broadcast to be received wherever television sets exist.

I was working in a London studio recently when I noticed a famous girl singer in the vocal booth on her own. I asked the engineer what was happening ... she was singing to a backing track which was being sent through a stereo digital telephone link from a Los Angeles studio, where the producer sat orchestrating the whole process. What would Bing Crosby have made of that I wonder!

I get telephone calls from live radio shows, asking me personal development questions usually, and this immediately gives me access to the homes of many thousands of listeners I have no other way of contacting *at the moment.* The Internet allows me to type, *and soon talk,* with people all over the place on sites like The World Forum. I watch and listen to the response people are making to these new developments, and it truly is an exciting time period in which to gather incarnate experience.

Yet, as I survive another surge of enthusiasm for all these new toys and tricks, I cannot help but contemplate the fact that they are all just physical harmonics of the spiritual capabilities on which we should really be concentrating. The more we rely on television, the less we will develop clairvoyance, clairaudience and telepathy. It is so easy to talk with someone on the telephone, yet it should be even easier to tune in with them mind to mind. The radio transmits into The Ether Waves and we listen using a receiver; would time be more lucratively spent tuning into the planet and beyond through meditation via those same Ether Waves? The Internet has given many of us an anonymous forum in which to pitch ideas for the contemplation of all, but I wonder just how much action stems from inspiration thus given.

Every single physical actuality has as its precursor, a thought. Each thought emanated from wherever, has spiritual impetus for it to have been contemplated in the first place. *As above so below; as below so above,* stated HERMES TRISMEGISTUS, *THE GREAT GREAT* and *MASTER OF MASTERS.* Is the sun, shining on all alike, a physical representation of The Solar System God, just as your body is the dense vehicle for you the spiritual being? I happen to feel that this is so, but you shouldn't believe me ... I don't wish to transmit beliefs to you ... you must sense for yourself, for this is the only effective personal development there is.

Intuitively sensing such to be the case however, allowed me to contemplate TELEVISION, TELEPHONE, RADIO AND THE INTERNET, just as they are. Inferior tools of higher potential which most of us have yet to touch. Now, I must be honest and tell you that I have yet to meet anyone who habitually gets every aspect of telepathy just right; which reminds me of just how many times television technology *didn't* work before it *did!*

In this era of instant gratification and fast this and that, it seems that if we do not see results from our efforts manifest immediately into our bank accounts, the action could not have been worthwhile. TELEVISION, TELEPHONE, RADIO AND THE INTERNET are all methods of being together, but their technologies have bypassed much more basic issues in their striving for world acceptance. There are few safeguards in place regarding ownership of the media, and countries to this day have their almighty and powerful media controlled by dictatorships. Thus, Libyans know only what they have been told through newspapers, television and radio, what their leader is like, and of course *he is the benevolent soul we all thought him to be,* as far as they are concerned.

It is not only third world countries who suffer this misinformation either. We are all at the capricious mercy of fiddlers with facts, manipulators of truth, weasels with words and politicians with elections to win. If you are truly dedicated to everlasting personal development, you have to begin looking behind the headlines and the obvious, for it is in so doing that you will discover that this world is far deeper and more mysterious than one may at first have thought. Pictures are powerful, because they demand the least from us in understanding them. Television is therefore the single most potent tool available to us for the furtherance of that honourable goal of *personal development for all!* There is no ring to the phrase *personal development for all* however. This world is run on buzz words and slick phrases; I would sense the yawns if I were to appear on national television with a soulful smile on my face stating my advertising slogan *personal development for all!* If I followed that slogan with a short explanation about the potential for human telepathy, there would be a surge on the national grid as kettles were boiled to fill a few million tea pots.

I have yet to discover, be informed of, read about, watch a television programme on or capture telepathically, any route to human perfection, that does not have in its engine room, *meditation*, as its power unit. Without employing meditation as the agent for growth, one would honestly miss a basic step which inevitably would have to be revisited in order for full understanding of what we are and where we are going, to exist. Television, fascinating and useful though it is, stops us from looking inward all the time we are looking outward at it, and relying on it for our view of the world. The telephone stops us from a mental concentration which would without doubt, eventually place us in touch with the subject and object of our telephone call; if that subject was also a willing participant, both of you would enjoy a toll free call. The radio is a little different as it does stimulate thought more readily whilst listening, but it infrequently allows participation ... this is why I participate and promote phone in type shows; they can be useful forums. Techno heads, byte junkies, computer freaks, anonymous authors and web weavers, in the main, are into computers, rather than being into what those computers can achieve for them. Recently, I logged onto a forum just as *all party talks* had once again begun in Northern Ireland, in an effort to re-establish peace. In a room of many people, only one typed positively to my request ... *all those willing to join me for a second right now in a positive thought for lasting peace in Ireland type yep!*

Meditation is linked to eastern religions by most of us here in the west. Yet it is not the domain of any single group or country. It is the one indelible right of all human beings to contact their home universe. Because of bigoted and prejudiced outlooks on this matter, I changed the title of meditation and called it *TTM,* or, *Time To Myself,* throughout all of my books. I have described various uses for it, but none of my words come even close to a useful description. The most inspiring I have ever come across, were the words of Krishnamurti; if they work for you, fine; if not, please persist in your search for the meaning of meditation, for it matters not where you get it from ...

> If you set out to meditate it will not be meditation. If you set out to be good, goodness will never flower. If you cultivate humility it ceases to be. Meditation is like the breeze that comes in when you leave the window open; but if you deliberately keep it open, deliberately invite it to come, it will never appear. Meditation is not the way of thought, for thought is cunning, with infinite possibilities of self-deception, and so it will miss the way of meditation. Like love, it cannot be pursued.

I enjoy TELEVISION, TELEPHONE, RADIO AND THE INTERNET, but

refuse to do so at the expense of our true spiritual potential. The physical aspects of life can exist side by side with their spiritual counterparts, until we all transcend the need for these tools which are less than inherent in us. I will conclude this bite with an invitation for you to begin compiling your mental *telepaphone* book of willing participants in human telepathy. I urge you as I urge myself, to have more TTM. Meditation is *just being,* and *just being* is what most of us are least good at. It therefore follows that if we are to indulge ourselves in personal development, meditation must receive priority if we are to lay relevant foundations for our onward progress.

THE EVIL OF PSYCHO SURGERY

Way back in 1976, I remember being involved in a campaign to end psycho surgery. I recall some of us even gathering outside cinemas where ONE FLEW OVER THE CUCKOOS NEST was being shown, asking people freshly moved by the unfairness of our outlook as a society on mental health, to support us. I wrote a song called *Ban Psycho Surgery,* which I wasn't allowed to record as I was under contract to a company who would certainly not have understood my sentiments, so it was recorded by someone else. Whatever happened to it I do not know, which means it mustn't have been a hit!

It wasn't until reading an article about The American Kennedy Family in the Sunday Times on 21 April 1996, that my interest was rekindled, albeit it in a very different way. The sub article was entitled *The casting out of a Kennedy daughter.* It said that Joseph Kennedy's second daughter Rosemary, JFK's sister, was slower than other children. As she grew older, her sweet disposition turned sour, and she often flew into uncontrolled rages. The Family would not tolerate losers and banned her from the house.

It seems it was decided that she was mentally ill, and as there were no drugs available to treat mental illness ... *nor are there any now I might add,* so old man Kennedy decided she would have a lobotomy, an operation pioneered in the 1930's, which I consider to be the most destructive addition to modern medicine ever considered. It involves severing the frontal lobes of the brain, which the neurological scientists originally did with monkeys in the 1930's. For Rosemary Kennedy however, it was thought to be potentially beneficial, even though she was not a monkey! Two Washington Doctors, Walter Freeman and James Watts operated during the autumn of 1941 ...

After she was mildly sedated, "we went through the top of the head," Watts recalled. He used an instrument like a butter knife swinging it up and down to cut brain tissue. As Watts cut, Freeman asked Rosemary questions. He would ask her to recite *The Lord's Prayer,* or sing *God Bless America.* When she began to be incoherent Watts stopped cutting. It became clear that the operation had made Rosemary's condition far worse. No one was told anything about it and she was removed to a Catholic nursing home in Wisconsin and never mentioned again inside or outside the Family. When news of Rosemary's condition finally leaked out during the sixties, the Family put it about that she had been born mentally ill.

Can you imagine being a part of that Family? Would you like to belong to an environment where winning takes precedence over people? As you can see, the general theme of this Bite is mental health, and that does not involve physically meddling with human brains. Another superbly devious ploy hatched by the PSYCHO PROFESSION was called ELECTRIC SHOCK THERAPY ... note an entirely illiterate use of the word therapy by this bunch of experimenters!

Such torture involves shoving a load of electricity through the brain via a couple of electrodes placed on either temple ... patients are sometimes found to be more mild mannered and timid after treatment ... one wonders why!

The human brain is not the same as a monkey's brain. You do not need qualifications to work this out. Just observe the outward behaviour of a human and then watch a monkey ... different eh! Nor would I condone the use of lobotomies or electric shocks on the animal kingdom either, but that is another subject.

Without a brain, there would be no consciousness after the marrying of spirit with matter. The human brain contains all the constituent parts of the animal brain, with the addition of brain bits that allow us to be human. We can look at how we think for instance, and question it. The neo cortex brain bit has provided us with the tool for telepathic communication. We are individualised spirit, whereas most of the animal kingdom, *to the best of my knowledge,* is a physical manifestation of various group spirits.

Ban Psycho Surgery, I wrote in 1976 ... it is sad to note that I am writing the same thing in 1996. I am the founder member of the POSITIVE ATTITUDE CLUB however, with the philosophy that all disasters contain within them opportunities for progress. Psycho Surgery was and is a disaster ... so what is the opportunity?

We can observe the blunders of the past and acknowledge them, without lingering on any kind of beautiful sentimental sadness which may be attached to this subject matter, before formulating a positive stride forward in our philosophy of dealing with our fellow humans. Raise a glass to Rosemary Kennedy by all means, along with all of the anonymous recipients of this demonstration of *man's inhumanity to man,* but understand that every time we *turn a blind eye,* or, *look the other way* and excuse our non intervention in the execution of a crime with the *I'm too busy* cliché, we delay the process of evolution.

Can that delay be measured?

In your own universe, *to the degree that you feel you are making a difference!*

THE HAUNTING OF CYRUS HIVANTREE

"Figuratively speaking," began the Lord Heavenly Father, "it takes a drunk to know a drunk; yet I know a drunk when I see one and I have never taken a drink in my life! I know a glutton when I hear one eating and I have not ever consumed so much as a leaf in the whole of my existence. In fact, I know everything there is to know, yet I know there is more to know than I know at present. It seems that I have perfected a world so full of paradox and equivocation, that even I stand in awe of my own creation every so often."

The Mind Divine mulled over its power, and stepped it down to such a degree in order for Cyrus to comprehend, that one could equate such dilution to the force of a water droplet, boiled and condensed to float away into the great cosmic vacuum. As this transference of sentiment was occurring, simultaneously, an emanation from the Heart Divine outpoured a sympathetic burst of the universal dint we call love. Those incarnations known as Initiates, tuned to the vibration for the purpose of de-tuning it, thus rendering it suitable for oft misunderstood earthly consumption by the masses. Cyrus had evolved midway between these two human capacities, and, confused by his power and lack of it, sometimes did good and occasionally did bad, with what he knew not quite.

"It is dangerous to know a little about a lot, but not a lot about a little," he thought. "What am I thinking about," he continued, "gobbledegook, gookledegob and nonsensical prose! Meter comes to me along with alliteration of which I have not a clue. From where do these ideas of which my head is full, emerge? Am I crazy? Am I normal and the rest of the world crazy? Does it matter? Perhaps I should content myself with something of which I am presently ignorant."

Cyrus Hivantree breathed out an audible sigh and inspected the old laurel bush at the end of his drive. Two years previous to this inspection, he had performed similar perception of an old English oak, before calling in tree surgeons to incapacitate it somewhat for the purpose of increased light to his abode, and a slight exercise of his corporeal domination over this elegant growth.

"Money for nothing," his thoughts continued, "money for rope and ropy old chopping job with saw from tree surgeons ... that's all I got and I could have done it myself which I shall this time! Save all my money and spend all I save, on savings of money buying rights which I waive. Peace begins with understanding."

Ever the problem with which Cyrus grappled, was the constant mixing of nonsense with inspirational messages; he borrowed a chain saw and assaulted the bush. The neighbours gathered around to observe. Most had not ever set eyes on Cyrus, who spent his time indoors with his thoughts and outdoors without thoughts. Thus, when he was in he was in, and when he was out he was out.

"Leave that bush alone," complained the man from over the lane, "what harm has it done you?"

"Is that Cyrus Hivantree who always cooks curry ... he is tall isn't he ... are they his children ... is that his saw ... his wife is pretty ... that's not his wife ... does he have permission to cut down the bush ... how will we all benefit ... more light ... less green ... prices will go up ... is he selling ... is it his ... he's a big chap ... mm, quite good looking!" The comments continued as did Cyrus, quite oblivious to them. He sweated and drank; on more than one occasion a curse passed his lips. "What did he say ... did I hear right

... uncouth and obscene ... I always knew ... you wouldn't expect that through looking at him!"

Two hours passed and his body began to shake. Inhalation of the two stroke fuel fumes caused breathing difficulties, and his hands were difficult to straighten from the grip moulded by the saw handle. He could take no more, and transiently noticed the audience of neighbours as he returned to the house for the purpose of telephoning a local tree surgeon to collect the vast amount of bush bits which had accumulated through his actions. In fact, he called the same tree surgeon whom he had last seen a couple of years earlier whilst administering surgery to the previously described elegant English oak.

"Where's he going now ... what's he doing ... cooking some curry ... nah he had that last night ... gone for a lie down ... he's weird." The comment and speculation fermented in the lane, but Cyrus did not again emerge that day, for he was ill. His body shook and his hands they tingled; his throat was dry and his knees they creaked. The physical exertion had quite literally forced his body into shock, and he was shocked to discover such weakness in himself. All the while, he thought; his shocked body enforced rest onto him. As he lay in bed day after day, he thought. Focusing ever so gradually with greater magnification, he came to know his thoughts, and soon began thinking them himself. As he began utilising this mind gift as it was intended, rather than the way it had imposed itself upon him, the gobbledegook and gookledegob disappeared and he began to create.

Cyrus began writing for no reason. "The tree surgeons practice tree surgery every day. This involves physical exercise and bravery, for some of those climbs they need to regularly make are awkward indeed. Their hands are strong and straighten easily after many hours holding a chain saw. In short, they have trained their bodies as I shall train my mind. Without a body however, I will cease owning a brain with which I am able to manifest my mind; I shall therefore attend to a degree of physical fitness and do justice to my new found mental capacity."

Cyrus Hivantree died very soon after that episode of his life involving the laurel bush, and long before he was able to fathom any real potential innate within his mental universe. Touched by a divine beam from the Heart of God, at the moment that silver chord of life was severed, making corporeal return impossible, he was aware of another latent capacity within himself. "What is this thing called love," he thought.

The One About Whom It Is Futile To Speculate

We were discussing the human soul and lack of concrete proof that exists to render it tangible for the six billion or so incarnate beings who are in varying stages of scepticism regarding it, and its exact nature. Our guide for the evening, whom we know as The Storyteller, mentioned an expectation of the Tibetan Master Djwhal Khul, transmitted through an Alice A Bailey book, that a Frenchman would discover concrete proof by the year 1975, thereby freeing humanity from further speculation of this type, perhaps allowing it to progress onto even more useful ventures.

Some of us are still speculating; I voiced the consternation that should such proof arise, maybe it would somewhat negate the process of self discovery ... *the intuitive sensing of the soul as that vital link between spirit and body*. I also verbalised concern that anarchy may result in a lessening of value being placed on *this* lifetime, in the knowledge that another is waiting just around the corner. I continued by wondering out aloud how a person who had not meditated or participated in much contemplation, would be fit enough to have this quick fix button pressed within.

A lady who was passing through our group, a transient participant, stated that she did not know why I was having such trouble with this subject; she was happy for concrete proof to arise, although unused to the nature of my questioning during such evenings. I asked for a consensus of opinion from everyone regarding the necessity for this proof. It was not met with an answer immediately; our guide for the evening looked on and listened, as do all the best guides. A Scottish lady asked if *I* believed such proof necessary and I replied that I had no beliefs or opinions ... an answer prone to make some uncomfortable.

I voiced the jarring question that others were also thinking, about spiritually non cognisant individuals being much *less* able than others who dutifully meditated and contemplated their way through life, and *this* questioning statement stimulated the revealing answers. Our guide stated that all incarnated beings were spiritually cognisant, and the quick fix button of concrete soul proof would merely turn on the light. The switch for that light is built into each and every one of us. The age old paradox concerning Esotericists looking on with woe, as their years of spiritual activity leave them behind, whilst previously disinterested people overtake them on the road to Nirvana, was then discussed humourously.

We laughed; but their was an amount of nervousness in our treatment of this topic. A lady who has been attending most of the Positive Attitude Club evenings since 1993, said that my meditation was a personal contribution to the whole, and not necessarily what each part of that whole has to be involved with. The guide added more to the concept of the human whole going forward together, and that further speculation about individual worth was futile. I began to cognite, which was the main purpose for the presence of us all that evening.

Historical context further enlightened me on the relevance of this question. We talked of Lemurian times, when humanity was developing the physical body; Atlantean times when that body was supplemented with mental and communication abilities like talking; to now, when, if we are to enter the fifth kingdom of spirituality successfully, the soul must be proved beyond question, just as was the physical body and mental abilities in eras now passed.

We do not question the body and its talent for thinking and verbalising the indwelling being's fiat; nor shall we question the soul within the very near future, and this will leave us free to explore heaven with greater freedom. When the soul looks down to the body we call it an ego, when it looks up to the spirit, we call it a solar angel. The soul straddles two great arenas just as the human body bestrides soulful and more concrete areas.

Perhaps our full entry into this spiritual fifth kingdom will allow us more purposeful speculation of THE ONE ABOUT WHOM IT IS FUTILE TO SPECULATE; for the time being however, let me affirm that it is in fact not futile to speculate about anything or body. Speculation is a close relative of contemplation, meditation and consideration; this troop of three thought processes are exactly what we should be doing as partakers of the mental universe, success in which for many of us, is a prerequisite for speedier access to fuller divinity. I write not about snap judgements and ill informed opinion ... I endorse speculation with reverence and creativity. The word futile refers primarily to our lack of ability to grasp the real meaning of Divinity, but this is an old, useless and outmoded idea of human capacity, about as worthwhile as is creating another sect, cult or religious division.

I also have lots to say concerning THE ONE ABOUT WHOM NOUGHT MAY BE SAID; perhaps you have too! This book however, concerns itself with THE ONE ABOUT WHOM EVERYTHING MAY BE WRITTEN. Whatever your God is called is good enough for me; if that were the universal case I am certain God, whatever it is, would be a lot happier. My speculation and long contemplation with this issue of Divinity has inevitably lead me back to one of my earliest feelings that I am as much a part of God as is God and yourself. What proof do I have? As much proof as we have about the presence of a human soul!

This is not to say that I am ubiquitous, omni-present, fully cognisant and presently all knowing in this incarnate state in which I find myself. The spark is there. The potential exists, and it is the working of this potential, the discovering of our latent abilities and sleeping capacities, that empowers us onward and ever upward. Just as our diminutive offspring have adult prowess awaiting them when maturity arrives, so too have we Divine power anticipating the dawning of each individual initiation.

Soul to soul I wish us both whatever proof we require for a fulfilled life of service and progress ...

THE THING ABOUT WHICH IT IS EXCITING TO SPECULATE

Written on the board was ALH 84001 ... *what does it mean,* we were asked. No one had a clue. It could have been medical jargon assigned by ICI to a new wonder cure for non specific urethritis or haemorrhoids, but it is in actual fact the code name given to a piece of asteroid found in Antarctica in 1984, on which proof that life had or does exist on Mars was finally discovered in 1996. If we are opening ourselves up to all potential, then this piece of valuable, scientific data helps enormously in our efforts to contemplate ourselves not only as one humanity, but also as some kind of giant universal family.

Much like proof of the soul can help tweak the already existent knowledge of who and what we really are, ALH 84001 is the first proof of life on other planets of which I am aware, potentially enabling contemplation within millions, of the bigger picture.

How long will it be before the life which has been proved from this piece of asteroid, is given three heads by the tabloids, a gross hunger for Indian virgins in a feature film, and the spin off TV series in which it is accidentally annihilated by an Iraqi nuclear bomb?

Not long!

Every single aspect of everything is endowed with consciousness. We tend to look at life exhibiting less consciousness than ourselves, with a domineering and patronising sneer, whilst viewing clever and more evolved life with respect and aspiration. There is in fact, no need to change our outlook on whatever we contemplate, for to do so is merely demonstrating opinion. Just what this life on Mars really is becomes of secondary importance to the fact that if life exists there, then just where does life end, if anywhere?

There are trillions upon trillions of galaxies and universes, star systems and solar systems, planetary connections and intergalactic alliances, evolutions, revolutions, convolutions and dissolutions; yet, within this ring pass not of contemplation, it is possible to be aware of yourself as a point of light; no greater or lesser than any of the grander descriptions which may be afforded other aspects of life ... just a simple point of light, having the choice of modus operandi, lifetime after lifetime.

Think of the stars and the space which exists between us all; see the space which lies between each and every atom comprising your body. Look at the space readily visible whenever a point of light like yourself views the heavens; feel the space existing wherever you may contemplate. Share the space, celebrate the space, join the space and journey in, on and around it.

Get the big picture whenever you feel yourself thinking small!

VACATIONS

How often have you heard friends say that they are taking a holiday to get away from themselves, their work environment or some other problem? People go to the hairdressers to execute change in their appearance. I see people buying new clothes to enhance their image, and purchasing bigger houses to exhibit an improvement in their status.

My advice is to take a vacation from all of the above and confront what is!

A new set of gnashers works a treat for the up front personality type recognition of physical improvement to the eye, and there is no doubt that such improvement can stimulate genuine mental development in a more knowing individual; but *new teeth* cannot ever mean more than *new teeth* in the long run. We have to maintain appearances, but if that means compromising your reality and neglecting everlasting potential then you best leave it out!

Personal development means never having to say you are sorry for something you did which meant no long term improvement for yourself or your sphere of influence. Real achievement is that which you can take with you once this physical lifetime has ceased. My advice is to take some time off from your habits and routines, and instigate some positive changes into your life which will fuel your bid for human freedom.

We all seem to walk around during this incarnation with a box around our heads. Those of you who may have seen the Box Of Illusions illustration we use for our personal development posters have an excellent point of reference to what I am writing about here. This illustration was taken from an original oil painting by Ginger Gilmour, a friend who shares similar outlooks on this *box thing idea* around our heads.

The box contains our outlooks and habits, mores and reactions, haves and have nots, wants and want nots, wheres and whereforenots. What usually happens ... all that we contemplate during consciousness is fed through this box before we allow ourselves perception of what by that time has become a weak harmonic of the original. The challenge we set ourselves in the PAC(K) and during other ventures of which I am part, is daring to discard the box, thus laying ourselves bare for all to see, *and for us to see all!*

You are not your habits or your illusions or your house or your feet or your family or in fact ... your map! The map with which you navigate life's paths is not the actual territory. You must ponder this philosophy a while and let it seep through the box. There is your map, another's map, usually a few million other maps, and then there is the actual landscape, viewpoint, feature, or communication you have been trying to negotiate ... usually with your map firmly in place, and willing to protect it in battle at whatever the cost!

This Illusion Box is nothing more than a conglomeration of all your karma; wins, losses, aspirations, let downs, loves, fears, murders, rapes, gives, takes ... need I write more? Some call it an aura, but it is not really the aura which I am discussing here. The Illusion Box can be ripped apart and its contents tipped into the garbage if you like. You can place another box over your head if you feel naked, or you can contemplate life without a box ... I dare you ... I really do!

Ponder on life without the box ... the territory as it is, and not as it has *seemed* to you. It is amazing just how many times you will catch yourself filtering a communication through your box, when you first begin to consider the possibilities.

Well, this is the best vacation I have on offer here at the

PAC(K) Travel Agency ... it's free and you don't need kennels for your dog ...

Do yourself a favour ... take a break from your box!

WHAT DOES BEING POSITIVE REALLY MEAN?

Different concepts of this notion are abound. No one can say whether one or more ideas are right or wrong. There are as many differing variations on understanding of positivity as there are human beings pondering the subject.

We have to accept that one can be positive about being negative for instance! Positivity in the contemplation of evil adds a thwack to potential destruction for sure. A positive outlook on *making yourself right at the cost of others,* will add weight to this miserable affliction also. Many of us are positive about our weaknesses, and this holds them nicely in place.

If the subject was easy, like flicking a switch, then evolution would advance accordingly. It isn't as simple as that however ... of that fact I am positive! Equally sure is the fact that each of us has a choice between being positive and negative, happy or sad, loving or fearful, good or bad ... and of course all the grades between each dichotomy ... before deciding what to do with that choice. Some people are even poor failures, whilst others fail magnificently!

PURPOSE is one aspect of the answer to pondering the above ... as Napoleon Hill said, *if you have no major purpose, you are drifting towards certain failure.* Mind you, I have often wondered why purposeless people do not drift towards certain success! It seems however, that they do not. Once you have a purpose, then it is a question how you go about the goals inherent within it. This is where the choice of good and bad must be made ... once that choice is made, then can POSITIVITY be added to the other ingredients of FAITH and DERTERMINATION, which must surely exist for any major accomplishment to occur.

You don't have to believe me ... just try it for yourself. Set yourself a small task like selling an unwanted piece of furniture through your local *Admag*. Firstly, think about the impossibility of selling this item ... how nobody would like to buy such a thing, it's too expensive and you may miss the telephone call from that one person who may want what you have got.

If you do not sell it, for we must understand that yours is not the only determinism involved in such a cycle of action, then place another advert; brimming with realistic confidence, visualise the purchaser, the cash, the time, date and location. Wait for your mental plan to materialise in the physical universe, constantly keeping your decision firmly in place and enforcing it with positive affirmation.

Whether or not you are successful of course, is entirely up to you. The nuances of mental attitude within each of us are so diverse, as to be literally impossible to define. That is why Personal Development authors like myself, work with certain common denominators, and in so doing always run the risk of being too general and vague, whilst usually attaining a preponderance of successful dissemination.

When you are triumphant, meditate on the insignificance of ALWAYS GETTING WHAT YOU WANT, and the superiority of its healthy cousin ALWAYS GIVING WHAT IS NEEDED! This type of outlook may not be very fashionable, hip, cool and right on, but it lasts forever, whilst lesser phases come and go.

Now do not think for a minute that I am not in absolute favour of YOU CAN ALWAYS GETTING WHAT YOU WANT; it is just that as a stage at the very beginning of any Personal Development, *getting what you want* can often entail a kind of blind affirmation that *No Matter What You'll Get It*. It only takes a small amount of contemplation to realise that this type of demand is so small minded and potentially destructive, that anything more than a brief flirtation with such sentiment will cause a karmic swirl which could render *you always being what someone else wants!*

Outflow equals Inflow ... the quality of outflow will eventually equal the quality of inflow ... like attracts like, and the biggest boost you can give yourself after honing the cutting edge of your life's story, or purpose, is to positivitise your outflow so it is doing so much good, that universal law decrees ... only good can come your way.

Try it for a lifetime and see how it goes!

WHAT IS THE LIGHT?

May I affirm this book as concentrating on the ever expanding subject of personal development! However, it is inevitable that there will be regular crossover points into spheres of the mysteries and esoteric philosophies often hidden from the masses throughout the ages. More information than ever before is now accessible to us, both through our own research, and because previously concealed hard data has become more readily available to aid this evolutionary stage in which we find ourselves.

Every single aspect of personal development is derived from a much stronger source of information. This is a fact which only gradually dawned on me as I emersed myself from the field of data in which I was engaged. Most information which you will discover about the mental universe, is derived from what Alice Bailey wrote about as *ENERGY FOLLOWS THOUGHT*. This has been adapted and simplified, others have taken credit for this startling and powerful bite of data, but it has its origins in facts recorded well before ages which historians are able to fathom.

What good the information gleaned from these mysteries can do us, is dependent on our intentions, for it can accomplish as much harm as it can benefit, even upon the unwary user of universal power for only *slightly* selfish gain. Magic has become acceptable to the world of self help and personal development in all but name. Newcomers to The Positive Attitude Club frequently claim their ability to reserve car parking spaces for themselves by *deciding* there will be one where they wish to park. I hear descriptions of the successful utilisation of small pyramid structures to keep razor blades sharp if stored beneath them. On the darker side, I know of perfectly normal, upstanding members of the community who claim to visit business colleagues on the astral plane during sleep time, to suggest a deal more beneficial to themselves than the unwitting colleague. They do these things and think this way because certain occult material has been slipped through their back door, so to speak, in a palatable format, from a medium such as personal development tapes, which has credence within their profession perhaps. They frequently do not want the whole story however!

I do.

For every action there is a reaction, and it seems that through utilising personal power for anything other than the good of others, unless you are well versed in artfully dodging the negative return for a while, a karmic kick could reach your backside sooner rather than later, to inform you that all is well with natural law. Celebrate your power, but bear this fact in mind when using it.

The Light, is a phrase bandied about for as wide a diversity of reasons as there are harmonics of THE SEVEN BEAMS FROM OUTER SPACE VIA THE MILKY WAY, as I described the seven rays of energy in my earlier book called EMPOWERMENT. Ultimately, I feel that *the absolute light* is unknowable at this present time, but as always in this field, we take a paragon and seek to emulate it. Light is just such an actuality. It is that which we all yearn for in some way, shape or form. Whether it be gradual illumination by a piece of data, or the sudden dawning of new horizons, as in a personal cognition or self realisation. Even switching on the light in a room! Without light there would be no life, and it seems that it is the amount of light which we can evoke into our lives which correlates with personal fulfilment of a true nature.

You will find yourself able to recite many phrases which have crept into human usage over the years which utilise this fundamental principle at their core ... *living in the light ... the light at the end of the tunnel ... I can just about see the light ... blinded by the light ... and then I saw the light ... the light dawned on me ...* and other less direct usage such as ... *white magic ... the white knight ... white witch ...* all opposite to ... *black magic ... and then darkness fell ... dark forces ... black death ... living in the shadows.*

The act of evolution is a path towards the light. If the sun is a physical emanation of the central spiritual sun, then just as corporeal life requires the bodily sun to shine its light, *which it shines on all alike,* so does the soul need to grow towards the spiritual paragon of light, just as a plant will bend, contort, and struggle its way towards the rays of the sun, which it cannot understand from a mental standpoint.

The light is also in its lesser harmonic, that spark of truth which exists within each of us; the spirit. THE GREAT UNIVERSAL LAW OF CORRESPONDENCE often allows an easier understanding of ourselves once we have embarked on this road called self improvement. If you can see yourself as a microcosm of something much greater and vaster, with all the potential of this macrocosm, then your point of light will be seen corresponding to the greatest point of light we are as yet able to vaguely comprehend; namely God, or whatever you wish to call your particular universal deity.

The *light* is you and me, and a brighter light is perhaps you and me together. It is not the lesser lights which exist within each and every particle of dust wherever they may be, but the light which sparks a human being into contemplation, of which I write, along with that greater light which we aspire towards and yearn to inspire of more. The first role of any personal development lesson is to signify that contact with your particular point of light must form the basis of all further personal development gains. Contact need not be vivid, and will without much doubt dawn gradually, but acknowledgement and an awareness of it must lie at the root of our future growth.

When I was introduced to a book called A TREATISE ON WHITE MAGIC, written by ALICE BAILEY and inspired by the Tibetan Master DJWHAL KHUL, my eyes firstly fell upon a set of words before the main body of writing began, with which I identified instantaneously. The sudden reverence I adopted towards these words was of interest to me, because they formed an invocation, which comprised part of a data area up until that time I had no interest in at all, along with prayers, mantras, evocations and chants. My work, some of which you are sampling here, is barely worthy of quoting the mentioned words. Of far graver concern to many will be the fact that I have adapted the words to, I hope, make them more suited to the age of sexual equality in which we find ourselves. Out of respect for the original, I have omitted the word *Great* from the title. To read the original however, I do recommend, and you will indeed find it in the already mentioned book, and many others.

The Invocation

From the point of light within the Mind Divine
Let light stream forth into human minds
Let light descend on earth

From the point of love in the Heart Divine
Let love stream forth into human hearts
May love surround the earth

From the centre where the Will Divine is known
Let purpose guide human goodwill
The purpose which Initiates know and serve

From the centre which we call the human race
Let the plan of love and light work out
And may it seal the door where evil dwells

Let light and love and power, restore The Plan on earth.

Who Is Your Doctor?
A person who has undergone a certain type of training ...

Much like a mechanic who studies engines and the workings of an automobile, a doctor considers the human body with varying degrees of cognisance. From initial studies, usually in a university and hospital, specialisation in particular types of bodily workings may occur, and much like the panel beater not knowing too much about carburettors, so the specialist will have a likewise field of vision centering only around his or her subject, and increased only with interest focused elsewhere.

I was born in 1953 to a working class family living in the north east of England. The Welfare State had been in existence since 1948 in Great Britain, and the idea of being looked after from cradle to the grave was indeed proving popular. Prior to this it was very much up to the individual whether or not to have treatment for any particular disorder, and much depended on the resources of that individual as to whether or not that answer was affirmative. This dissuaded many from pursuing medical treatments, and as often as not the bodies innate self curing mechanisms together with Auntie Willa's herbal remedies, did the trick without undue amounts of attention from all and sundry.

Of course, it also must be noted that advances in medicine and education had increased both life expectancy and the quality of that elongated life, so, as with all that we contemplate, a balance must be achieved in our viewpoints about the whys and wherefores of the medical profession. It is such imbalance that this writing addresses.

You see, doctors were afforded a kind of god like status, with the power of life and death, comfort-discomfort, high and low, and whatever other pairs of opposites come into your mind regarding the human condition. What the doctor recommended, or in many cases ordered, prescribed or forbade, became an immutable law of the individual's universe. As this platform of altitude was noted by doctors, the ratio of rudeness and irreverence for the patient's viewpoint grew.

In many cases, an individual could actually be heard defending the general practitioner's irascibility as part of the necessary personality a person of such high honour required. As dependence on the doctor grew, the patients accepted less and less responsibility for their own cases. As the piscean age faded, and some of us experimented with drugs, sex, rock and roll, freedom of speech and demonstrations, it occurred to many of us that these people of medical esteem did not seem to be advancing according to the call of the aquarian age which is now upon us.

If it was not in last week's medical journals then it wasn't true. Prescriptions were written according to the adverts placed in doctors' favourite journals, by the drug companies. It seemed that world domination would not be brought about by governments ... this opportunity would be presented to the drug companies. ICI, Glaxo and many others controlled what pill you would be slipping down your unsuspecting throat next. The doctors' work loads grew unrealisable and the public got educated.

Why did the general practitioners know so little about herbs, chiropractic, osteopathy, naturopathy, homeopathy, salts, crystals, universal energy, acupuncture, but most of all the most ubiquitous killer of them all ... *the psychosomatic illness!*

Yes my friends, self imposed ailments compose perhaps ninety percent of the conditions you take to your general practitioner. As Jules Verne said in the nineteenth century ... *if you can conceive it, you can achieve it!* Few actually consider the downside of this power however. Thoughts are things, and whatever you consider to be ... is! If you have no control over your thoughts, it follows that whatever passes through your mind and grabs your attention, will in actual fact control your life. Listen to people talking; they will normally relate what is spoiling their lives within the first few sentences of a communication to you. Such verbal communication will be a direct result of their thoughts. Most doctors do not know this.

Like everything that comes into being, it is first thought by an artist and often scolded by a scientist. Yet, as we find ourselves travelling further into this aquarian age, it will be noted that increased time will be spent by men of science dealing with the more mystical elements of life, as a route towards the knowledge we require to catapult us forward along life's evolutionary way. Science can only take us on a small part of our journey; the mental universe is a more advanced portion of the path which hopefully will lead us upward and ever onward towards the spiritual universe, which I am sure is comprised of almost unlimited strata.

Before I diversify uncontrollably into a treatise on evolution, let me ask you this ... how much can you really trust a doctor who you know only from a limited number of brief mutually shared time spans? You will know little of the doctor's socialisation process, almost nothing about the thoughts which comprise the doctor's mental universe; you'll have scant knowledge of the shares which your doctor owns, which may influence a decision towards prescribing drugs manufactured by a partly self owned company. This list could get very long. The point I am making is that your doctor is such a small part of your welfare programme that most of us should not ever need to visit one in the course of a whole lifetime.

As we move towards such a state of affairs, general practitioners should make themselves far more cognisant of *patient power,* and disenfranchise themselves of the idea that if it is not made by ICI then certain death will be the result! They need to read and practice new ideas; ask their patients to *think* themselves well; challenge age old belief systems and rid themselves of scientific bigotry.

Even now, approaching eighty five percent of medical procedures and surgery are scientifically unproved, more people are killed by medical practitioners than firearms in the United States and it is gauged that doctors are three times more lethal than guns! It is up to the medical profession itself to instigate reform, and it is pressure from words like these which propel often sedentary progress forward at a more rapid rate. This is not an attack on doctors, it is an appreciation of the potential which such people have at their disposal. We should understand their limitations and utilise them accordingly.

Who is your doctor? This is a complex question which I hope you never need to seriously ask!

WHY ARE SO MANY OF US SKINT?

Yet another piece of literature has arrived, which asks those of us with money to send a little more to a particular appeal, thereby helping those without. I used to enjoy contributing, but I no longer feel that sentiment. I look beyond and wonder how I can help those who cannot contribute through lack of funds, to get funds so they *can* contribute, and onwards to help those whom the appeal is intended to aid in the first place.

This business of personal development sure has deep implications for any of us willing to dive into the water to see how deep it is. I don't think you help anyone by excusing their lack of resources ... just as much as you cannot ever judge a person by their scarcity of means, or indeed their abundance of cash. I see too many so called spiritually oriented people relying on those of us who have financially prepared for life in this physical universe. It should not be this way. We should all rely on ourselves, and our interdependence with others, to supply us with whatever we need to live a holistic life style during incarnation, without ever resorting to appeals, begging and other more duplicitous and *round the back door* type ways of asking for money.

The churches are a solid example of straightforward *pay as you pray* type asking, with their collection trays ... *watch the eyes on you as you try and slip your meagre contribution onto a tray which someone else has endowed with a more weighty gesture.* The esoteric organisations ask for contributions but seem happy to keep you on their mailing lists whether or not you respond positively. This is in keeping with the agreement that one never charges for guidance in the ageless wisdom ... meaning that to change semantics and ask for contributions by another method is okay? Christian aid accomplishes much and would achieve even more if it dropped the sectarian part of its title and gathered funds without advertising its religious orientation.

Cancer, children, animals, m.e., m.s., m.*whatever,* and a whole host of similars, are just waiting around the corner to gobble up whatever you have, in the name of some cause or other, that someone has been moved to begin.

What is the point of these words? As long as the money comes in one way it will rarely by sought by another. If cancer is funded by donations then it will not be financed by government. Because lifeboats are now proud of their voluntary donation identity, they will not ever receive a budget from the Navy. I could cite many more examples, but all that I write has the purpose of impacting the individual and not the group ... in the first instance.

If your mother cooks your meals then you won't. If your father gives you money then that is the exact amount less than you will have to earn yourself. We need to get real and face up to the situation that lack of money is the result of a singular deficit of thought on that subject in the right direction. You can put your energy into ways of begging for money, or the exact same amount of energy into a method of earning that money yourself.

I propose the latter to be more beneficent in the long term!

Many of us are skint because that is how we think. We use a scarcity mentality to run around telling all and sundry how poor we are in the hope of a charitable handout. This equation is further complicated by the fact that we must *retain* a large degree of charity whilst implicating this most capitalist of ideas concerning *self thought wealth* into practice. There are further anomalies ... the running of a country for instance, when services only utilised by few need to be subsidised by many. Loss making branch railway lines for instance, that comprise part of the infrastructure of a country; is a country not less well off without them regardless of their financial inviability?

Criminals are another class of human to ponder over when thinking about money. Some of the cleverest people around have chosen the negative way to what appears as happiness; in esoteric circles they would be thought of as travelling the left hand path, and of course it is obvious that anything achieved without personal effort which includes pain of one kind or another to fellow human beings, must be paid for at some other time ... this is a karmic part of the equation.

Just as you can think your way to an abundance of money, the opposite must also be true ... Napoleon Hill's *Think and Grow Rich* book could just as easily have been called *Don't Think Yourself Poor!*

Of course you must also consider that, like an untended garden grows weeds and haphazard bits and pieces, so does a neglected thought pattern in the mind produce anarchy. You must manage your money thoughts better than most of us mismanage our bank accounts; unless you think the right financial thoughts, you will have no need of the banks, building societies, friendly societies, assurance companies, endowment agencies or indeed any other institution that lays claim to being the best place to deposit the physical manifestation of your financial thought processes.

By all means *think and grow rich,* but let me add a curve by telling you that if money is the object of your desires then it will rarely be forthcoming along with happiness. As I stated in YOU

CAN ALWAYS GET WHAT YOU WANT ... *happiness arrives during the accomplishment of an otherwise unrelated goal*. Likewise, money flows in to the degree that your attention is on an otherwise unrelated purpose. All you need do is ensure that you dedicate your actions to an honourable goal which society has deemed worthy of much financial gratification.

Priests don't make much; successful actresses do. Waiters are mostly poor; restaurant owners are more likely to be rich. It also must be said that there are many people living in abject poverty who are right on purpose and happy as their karma allows ... ascetics and perhaps Buddhist monks being good examples?

Look at all angles, and above all feel a sense of duty towards the achievement of wealth. So much good can be accomplished with money, and I honestly believe, as I have written before, that for the vast majority of us it is easier being spiritual with a pound in our pockets than it is when we are destitute and looking for our next meal. I frequently remind the Positive Attitude Club, just before we gather to creatively discuss some far out topic or another, of just what a privileged position we are in ... we discuss the finer aspects of existence whilst others are dodging terrorist bullets and famine.

I would rather spend time planning what I am going to do with a million pounds, than waste time thinking positively about how poor I am.

What do you think?

Words and Language

What can an English Personal Development author offer immigrant communities? Who knows? Lots I would think. The real question is whether or not we are willing to explore the interdependent potential between communities for the enhancement of each? The answer to this question in my universe is forever affirmative! If you can see the benefits of sharing in this manner then read on ... if not then I hope you read on anyway out of curiosity.

As a dedicated personal development author, I write regularly, and if I am to be increasingly effective, you must willingly feedback to me information regarding the potency of these bites. Are you? I don't mean just sitting back and thinking the feedback; if you are to impact the world in any way, shape or form, this requires action; good action is precipitated by positive thought. I run The Positive Attitude Club, as leader of the PAC(K) ... which is an acronym for Positive Attitude Club. Perhaps therefore, I am in a position to share with you my experience, which has been gathered over the years through continuous flirtation with personal development, but I do this with an eye on interactivity, which requires a contribution from you.

My bite for you on Words and Language is brief, and concerns a simple personal experience. In 1977, my wife and I rented a room to a lady freshly arrived from Gujarat in India, who had enrolled on a course of spiritual development which was regularly held not one mile from where we lived. She was a bright lady who had the good fortune to immediately fall in love with a German taking the same course. They married, both utilising the surname Patel, much to the intrigue of the German's parents more accustomed to the Schmidts and Beckanbauers of this universe.

She struggled on this course, and the fundamental aspect of her problem lay with the language. We all have differing ways of both thinking and communicating; the three principal modes are visual, auditory and kinaesthetic, the latter word is connected with feeling and motion. This lady *thought in words,* and as her native language was Gujarat, although she spoke and wrote excellent English, she found it necessary to translate her studies continuously, and in order to do this she required an *excellent* dual language dictionary, which at that time was not available in this country, nor in India, as she discovered to her cost when returning there for the purpose of buying one, to no avail.

Words allow us glimpses of concepts which remain unstimulated within us until prompted by the relevant expression. Let me share with you my transmission of this idea which I utilised in my second personal development book which is called BEFORE THE BEGINNING IS A THOUGHT ...

> Should I ask if you enjoyed gnoating, you could not tell me, as gnoating is not part of your vocabulary. You would be unable to conjure up a picture of this pastime I call gnoating. This means that gnoating would be one avocation unavailable to you consciously. Behind every word is an idea. The more words you understand, the greater amount of ideas you will be capable of enjoying. Your mental lexicon is a direct contributor to your accomplishment ability in all it's forms. You must add to it routinely!
>
> If I asked you to gnoat with me, and you placed your arms around my waist ready to dance, I could laugh or be offended. If I was shy I may avoid you in the future. If I lacked decorum I might engage verbiage in an effort to return the offence. You see gnoating does not have any connection whatsoever with dancing. You would have a misunderstanding of the word gnoat, and

thus the action of gnoating.

If you doubt your understanding of any word then consult its definition in a good dictionary. The most important tools with which you must equip yourself for your new future are the very best dictionary that money can buy, stimulating books and aware people. The derivation of a word can be particularly useful to your understanding of grander concepts, and all good dictionaries will show these etymologies. The greater your vocabulary, the easier your passage to success through natural philosophy will be.

For the record, there was no such word as gnoating, so I have invented both it, and its meaning. I define it as follows: Gnoating ... the act of passing a word that you do not understand without referring to a dictionary and clearing the meaning of that word fully with yourself. Slang: dullard; illiterate; dolt; person lacking brightness.

Don't be a gnoat ... get a dictionary!

As you may gather from the foregoing example, this problem does not only lie with people who utilise their second language most of the time. It is a challenge we all must face in our yearning to realise full human potential. As one begins to contemplate the finer aspects of existence, it further become apparent that the language you spent so much time mastering, is not able to summarise the concepts which require description. For the time being however, language and words are the tools we must use to improve ourselves.

If you learned 1 new word per day, 7 per week, 196 per month, approximately 2,360 per year, can you imagine the realms in which your thoughts would be able to dwell, with such a constantly improving vocabulary? Statistically speaking, such a word store would make you super literate, and a member of the *upper ten percent of the top two percent* of society likely to be incredibly successful in life. All this for taking the time to define one new word each day!

Reading for enjoyment is fine, but the words that I share with you are designed to stimulate action. I therefore feel it necessary to ask you as I did in a previous bite, if you have passed any words in this article so far that you do not fully understand. Go on, cast an eye back to the beginning and have a look through. If you have passed some *not understood* or *misunderstood* words, then note your weakness to so do, and remedy this in future by clearing every word you do not fully understand.

Now, it has to be said that this bite is a little on the dry side. It contains little entertainment value and no personality type tricks on how to get one over on fellow members of humanity. As you may have gathered so far into the book, this is where I am quite rightly coming from. I hope you like the style, and if not, I hope you are willing to ignore it and perhaps by just concentrating on the sentiments contained herein effect some decisive long term impact into your life which will change it for the better. I do not preach that such change is easy, as many writers do. I make no promises about anything.

You are the only person in this whole universe who is able to improve yourself. This is a huge responsibility, and you have taken a big step by involving yourself with my well intentioned words, if, you are willing to put these words and your understanding of them into action. Well ... are you?

YOU AND SERENDIPITY

This word serendipity was first coined by Horace Walpole during the eighteenth century, after characters in that fairy tale, The Three Princes Of Serendip; the princes in that story possessed the faculty of *making fortuitous and unexpected discoveries by accident*. This is indeed an excellent trait for any human to possess, and it seems belief that such *fortuitous and unexpected discoveries* are available for us all to make, renders them even more likely to happen. It therefore follows that it would help onward progress if we were to render our minds and being, susceptible to this remarkable potential of serendipity.

Many of us fall into a self made trap of seeking sympathy for a mythical situation which surrounds us, of hopelessness and sickness, and of course this type of thought frequently turns out to be of the self fulfilling prophecy variety. Equally, one may choose to fill a personal universe so brim full of positivity and serendipity, that the thoughts once made demand success from their physical universe counterparts.

Think virtuous thoughts and benefits will come your way... expect the finest and excellence will be forthcoming... seek light and you will see light ...search out success and you will discover it.

I remember when PeRFECT WORDS and MUSIC began trading; the outlay was so great in the first while, that I began to sense a feeling of foreboding whenever mail fell onto the mat. I expected bills, difficulties and even insurmountable obstacles ... this line of thought began to impinge on my sphere of operation until I nipped it right in the bud. I decided that we already were successful, at which point the whole atmosphere improved, thus allowing us to continue progress in a more enjoyable way. I know of many instances where people have thought themselves broke ... low and behold it happens for them just as they had thought.

Now, there is a trap in this line of conviction, and it is to just think the thought and do nothing else about it. Perhaps when willpower is strong enough, which will be in the future for most of us, this will indeed be enough, but for the time being it seems action is also needed to expedite your thoughts into physical actuality.

There is also a danger of leaving things too late, and connecting up with the wrong people, which is what the 103 year old man on his deathbed realised. He called on his wife to hear his dying words.

"Ethel," he said, "you have stuck by me through thick and thin; we were born into poverty and we married stony broke. We had four children in four consecutive years and they damn near finished us off. When our first born died, you stood by me in my abject misery; and then the war ... 1914 until 1918 ... I came back wounded and almost finished, yet you tended my every need. The depression arrived; I was without work for ten whole years and you didn't leave me. You were at my side during the Blitz when that roof collapsed on my leg leaving me lame, and you have stayed with me ever since.

As I lie here dying Ethel, I am just wondering if you are not just a bit of a jinx!"

I remember studying Viktor Frankl's work on human response to certain impulses, which he called Logotherapy. Whilst he was interned by the Germans in a concentration camp during the second world war, suffering unspeakable conditions, he noticed that when someone reported the imminent arrival of liberating allied forces after listening to an illegal radio receiver, a colleague of his showed more life and spirit than had been the case before. When the time passed without that event occurring, and rumour spread that it wouldn't happen for a much longer time, and there was even uncertainty about that, this colleague actually died of *hopelessness!*

If you can die of hopelessness, you can also live with optimism! In fact, and I have not ever come across any denial of what I believe to be the case, it seems that the more you think yourself a certain way, a kind of destiny is declared around that thought, like an almost imperceptibly weak harmonic of the initial creation of our universe. It has to happen!

Many other factors will find their way into your equation however, and it is usually these ingredients which allow doubt to creep in and weaken the initial thoughts, which then turn against their conceiver, working in the same fashion as would their positive predecessors, had they been thought a little stronger.

I believe that the whole of evolution is based around the universal law of serendipity. *Fortuitous and unexpected discoveries* are waiting just around the corner for those of us who are now realising the power of thought, just like weaker harmonics of much greater universal happenings. The ancient Hermetic axiom already mentioned earlier in this book, *as above, so below; as below, so above,* holds true here as in all other aspects of life.

You have to do it though! It is no good reading these sentiments and sensing inspiration without putting it into practice. You have to explore your thinking patterns and have the fortitude to stop any unproductive habits which have crept in through the back door over the years. In my experience, this is not an overnight phenomenon. Yet, each new plateau which is reached, creates enough of an impulse to climb higher at the next try ... but you have to actually do it!

Just like the comic books of the early 1900's, along with H G Wells and Jules Verne, describing space flights and trips to the moon, only dreams at the time but in actual fact evolutionary destinies ... I wonder if the writer of The Three Princes Of Serendip realised that this fairy tale was in actual fact based around a fundamental universal postulate of *fortuitous and unexpected discoveries available for us all!*

Probably.

YOU CAN ALWAYS GET WHAT YOU WANT TOO

I have been asked many times if I still feel that my first book is as relevant now as it was when I wrote it back in 1993. The answer is *no*; it is probably more relevant, now that even greater numbers of people are facing up to the fact that there is more to life than meets the eye, and sales reflect this fact accordingly as more of us step onto the first rung of the personal development ladder.

However, it is plain from the mini surveys which we take from time to time, that many people to whom my work is presented through this first book, are sometimes a little bewildered by its successors, unlike those who have been introduced further up the line so to speak, who immediately appreciate where I am coming from, as they deliberately purchased books and tapes after perusing their content, rather than just buying another product by the same author.

Some PAC people asked me recently why I did not stay with the YOU CAN ALWAYS GET WHAT YOU WANT type material; I asked if they would have enjoyed a regurgitation of the same concepts using different analogies and metaphors, perhaps called YOU CAN ALWAYS GET WHAT YOU WANT TOO. The reply surprisingly was *affirmative,* and this made me think!

Am I writing for myself, or do I spend all this time and effort presenting material for others? Are commercial pressures such that I must follow the way of the world with new work only slightly different to that which I have already presented, much like a new compact disc from the latest pop group which you could swear you had heard somewhere before, or should I follow my instinct and allow my work to evolve along with personal progress and self realisations.

Well, you may have guessed that I have chosen to *evolve,* both personally, and professionally in my work, which inevitably means that a few loyal reader and listener friends have been alienated along the way. It was either this course of action, or *contriving* books and tapes for the market place; there are shelves groaning under the weight of such fodder, and it seems you have veered away from it and purchased this work ... I hope you are pleased with the method of stimulation these bites have been designed to present!

The object of all my writing is to make you and I think together, and this cannot occur if I insist on bombarding you with facts and knowledge, which could have the effect of leaving you stale and uncognitive. It is inevitable that I have moved on from the first book, which is *the body* of a trilogy, to the second, which represents *the mind,* before prematurely concluding with the third, which is *the spirit*. I then continued with the fourth, under an assumption that *this world is not made from atoms ... it is built with stories*. Now, I offer this random selection of bites, or small pieces of thought provoking inspiration, which should continue the holistic story which you and I are starring in together, as an aid to self realisation, which I believe to be the only true way forward.

I do not involve myself with large seminars, which undoubtedly gross big money for their presenters ... I do not endorse any aspect of life which is at variance with my own beliefs, even when this could mean big money once again. I do not follow up a successful product with another just different enough to be classed as new. I do not compromise with my reality at all! I do not write one way and live another ... although it has to be said that some aspects of my life need to catch up with my written offerings. I do not preach perfection and live life without aspiration towards such idealism.

I live my talk, and this means that the only YOU CAN ALWAYS GET WHAT YOU WANT TOO available is this one you are reading now! It has been tempting ... I like the play on that word two, into too, meaning *as well as* ... but, no matter how I wrestled with the idea, a title like YOU CAN ALWAYS GET WHAT YOU WANT TOO would always transparently have the intention behind it, to hoodwink readers of the original YOU CAN ALWAYS GET WHAT YOU WANT into buying its follow up. No sir or madam!

Respecting all concerned with this particularly personal bite, anyone hooked on the first book, unable to grasp the importance of moving onwards and upwards ever, is missing a fundamental component of all true personal development. A UNIVERSAL LAW which states that NOTHING STAYS THE SAME; *it either gets better or it gets worse!*

Wins stimulated from the first book will be stale by now, if they have not be succeeded by *personally conceived* improved and better ideas, which the following books and tapes are designed to stimulate within you. This is the plan, but not *The Plan* however, which is the only Plan I know which *is* perfect. So we are dealing with a less than perfect plan which requires more input from you than you may at first imagine. In the short term, and in line with the old Rolling Stones classic, you *can't* always get what you want anyway. In any term getting what you want always involves giving, or providing a service for others, usually way over and above what all around are willing to supply. To get what you want from life you must ask yourself if you are willing to pay the price.

I habitually think long term, allowing deferred gratification to blend with an amount of instant gratification, serving my personality and the soul in a balanced viewpoint of winning for all in whatever I touch as a human being. I *can* always get what I want. If you think the right thoughts and do the right actions, with a flexible plan and an holistic approach to all you do and say ... YOU CAN ALWAYS GET WHAT YOU WANT TOO!

I therefore urge you to ...

GO AND SUCCEED TOO

The Positive Attitude Club

Madeira, Hunts Road, St Lawrence, Isle of Wight PO38 1XT

IF YOU WOULD LIKE TO JOIN WITH US

WELCOME TO THE CONSTANTLY EVOLVING PAC CONCEPT

The Positive Attitude Club accepts applications from anyone able to contemplate beyond the obvious. All we ask is that they embrace the philosophy that positive attitudes are helpful. This is a member's organisation; direction, activities and content ideas are always welcome. In line with our plans for the expansion of this beautifully simple philosophy, every member is invited to begin their own local PAC along the lines of *forward thinking through creative discussion*. In harmony with my own Mission Statement, I shall be available for as many activities as are practical to my own schedule. Large or small, old or young . . . all becomes irrelevant when immersed in inspirational interdependence!

Name ....
Address ....
....
.... Post Code ....
Telephone ....
Date of Birth ....
Occupation ....
Contribution ....

towards seasonal newsletter, meeting costs and general administration

Membership Number . . . . . *to be allocated* . . . . .

Let's enjoy toady whilst looking forward to a rosy future

Naturally, I hope you join with us. I also feel it important to point out my experience that many people join expecting something which it seems the PAC does not always deliver. I therefore here affirm that the PAC is only what *you* make of it; how can it be any other way unless Phil Murray turns it into some kind of personality oriented group encouraged into existence for his benefit only. You can make a difference, but not just by following *what is* already.

We look forward to being influenced by you!

Phil Murray
Leader of the PAC, 1st January 2000

PAC is an acronym for Positive Attitude Club

The PAC philosophy states simply that improvement of personal life through positive attitudes benefits humanity as a whole. We are an independent non-profit-making organisation dedicated to peaceful interdependence through creative discussion and forward thinking for the world.